The LIFESTYLE of the CROSS

The LIFESTYLE *of the* CROSS

Dr. Robin A. Riggs

EQUIP PRESS
Colorado Springs, Colorado

The LIFESTYLE of the CROSS

All Scripture quotations, unless otherwise indicated, are taken from the Holy Bible, New International Version®, NIV®. Copyright ©1973, 1978, 1984, 2011 by Biblica, Inc.™ Used by permission of Zondervan. All rights reserved worldwide. www.zondervan.com The "NIV" and "New International Version" are trademarks registered in the United States Patent and Trademark Office by Biblica, Inc.™

Contents

Acknowledgements   7
Introduction   9

1. Christ's Terms for Discipleship   11
2. On the Way to the Cross   18
3. Bearing the Cross   29
4. The Message of the Cross   41
5. The Wisdom of God   60
6. Portraits of Christ   69
7. Crucified with Christ   80
8. Not I, but Christ   88
9. Crucified in Weakness, Living in Power   97
10. The Difference Is the Cross   103
11. Sharing the Sufferings   108
12. Some Perspective on Suffering for Christ   117
13. Whatever It Takes   131
14. Enduring the Burden   139

Appendix   146

Acknowledgements

I wrote this book over many years. It began as an idea in my mind in the late 1970s, and later that idea was developed into Sunday school lessons. During my first pastorate I further developed the idea into a series of sermons, and finally decided to expand it into book form. I worked on this book's concept "in the cracks" of my busy schedule; however, this gave the opportunity for the message to "cook." I finally finished the final revision during the summer of 2015. I lived with the ideas in this book all those years, and they affected my ministry and preaching. Many people have read excerpts of the manuscript or the manuscript in its unfinished stages. Most of these people were members of congregations I pastored. These brothers and sisters in Christ constantly encouraged me to finish and publish what they deemed a worthy message. I appreciate all the urging along the way. It didn't speed me up, but it did help inspire spurts of writing activity over the years.

Most of all I want to thank my wife, Sheila, and children, Xen and Shayla. They have always encouraged me in my ministry endeavors, and cheered me on as I wrote. Sheila especially kept me motivated to keep on track and expressed her excitement that I finally had a finished work ready to be publish. Sheila has ever been essential to my sense of purpose, whether I was writing, working toward my doctorate, or going about pastoral ministry. She is my partner in every sense of the word, and I don't know what I would do without her comfort, encouragement, and her belief in me. God certainly knew what He was doing when He put us together.

I give thanks to God for the message he put in my heart. It is not entirely novel; many have preached and taught the truths in this book. But this is my own thinking about these things and my own words placed on paper over the years. I pray the result will affirm a very crucial message to the people of God and speak to their hearts as they follow Jesus on His terms.

Introduction

The message of the gospel of Jesus Christ is one of grace, forgiveness, salvation, change, and hope. It promises a new start for everyone who believes. It is the ultimate positive message. Because of that, it has been adopted and co-opted by many causes—political, social, philosophical, and religious. It has been used by teachers of positive thinking and by preachers of social transformation.

In a day when theologies of prosperity and success have been so popular, it seems fitting to re-emphasize the place of the cross in the Christian lifestyle. This book will undertake a (by no means exhaustive) discussion of the biblical norm for Christian living as we look at the terms of discipleship set forth by Jesus Christ.

But what is the heart of this gospel? What did Jesus teach and stand for? The core of the gospel is the message of the redeeming power of the cross of Christ. It is a picture of both suffering and victory. Both elements are absolutely necessary to the message. Some have chosen to emphasize the suffering side, reveling in ideas of revolution and martyrdom. Others have chosen to emphasize the victory of the cross, even suggesting that being a Christian is the solution to all of one's problems. But the message of the cross must not be deprived of either of these aspects, and their proper balance must be taught, or else the message is distorted from that of the New Testament.

The life of discipleship is a lifestyle based on the message of the cross. Therefore, "the lifestyle of the cross," as I am using that term, is one that contains both elements of suffering and victory. But what kind of suffering, and what does that victory look like?

The assertion of this book is that genuine Christian discipleship is defined by the message of the cross, and that message is defined by the life, death, and resurrection of Jesus Christ as portrayed in the New Testament. No one has the prerogative to define Christian discipleship for him or herself. When we follow Christ according to our own notions of what that means, or what we want it to mean, we will "invent" a kind of discipleship that is different from that which Jesus would approve. Jesus Himself declares to us the terms of following Him. That is what the following chapters seek to discover and explore. As we come to terms with what the Bible says about discipleship, we must be prepared to be strictly honest with ourselves and ready to modify (or even overhaul) the manner in which we are claiming to follow Christ.

The cross of Christ is the foundational truth for Christian living. Throughout this book, when "the cross event" is spoken of, it includes both the crucifixion and resurrection of Christ as comprising one complete event.

Chapter One

Christ's Terms for Discipleship

We cannot be Christ's disciples on any other terms except those declared by Christ Himself. Jesus' terms are summed up in His words in Luke 14:27: "Whoever does not carry their cross and follow me cannot be my disciple." That is very straightforward, but what does it mean?

Many popular teachings emphasizing prosperity, success, and self-fulfillment have paid too little attention to cross-bearing as a necessary condition for Christian discipleship. Jesus plainly asserted that cross-bearing is indispensable to following Him. Any version of the Christian life that fails to insist on this aspect of discipleship is based on a diluted gospel, if only because of the importance Jesus Himself placed on cross-bearing for discipleship. Part of the lack of attention to cross-bearing is due to a distorted understandings of its meaning.

The ministry that the modern church often designs for itself is not always the ministry of Christ. It is wonderful for a church to aspire to be busy, social, well thought of, and accepted. But we often plan ministries and activities in our churches that are basically risk-free. We want a positive public image, and we sometimes work for that and try to preserve it to the detriment of an honest and fully biblical witness in the world. We don't want to offend lest potential attenders and supporters are turned away from our meeting-house doors.

Yet Jesus and Paul both made it plain that in order to make the gospel pleasing to the ears of unsaved men and women, its real message about sin and the need for salvation must often be compromised. Paul wrote in 1 Corinthians 1:21-25, "For since in the wisdom of God the world through its wisdom did not know him, God was pleased through the foolishness of what was preached to save those who believe. Jews demand signs and Greeks look for wisdom, but we preach Christ crucified: a stumbling block to Jews and foolishness to Gentiles, but to those whom God has called, both Jews and Greeks, Christ the power of God and the wisdom of God. For the foolishness of God is wiser than human wisdom, and the weakness of God is stronger than human strength." If the message of the cross appears foolish to the world, the life that is lived on the basis of that message (what I have termed "the lifestyle of the cross") will be deemed equally foolish to the world. In 1 Corinthians 1:17, Paul wrote that God sent him "to preach the gospel—not with wisdom and eloquence, lest the cross of Christ be emptied of its power."

The word "gospel" means "good news." It is a message that says that all have sinned and need to be saved. The bad news of the sinfulness and lost condition of the soul must be shared in order to get to the good news of the offer of salvation. In this sense, the gospel cannot be made inoffensive to the world and still remain the gospel. Sin must be addressed in order to communicate the offer of salvation. It is the nature of sinful men and women to resent a light that exposes their sin and does not approve it, but instead calls upon them to forsake it.

The Christian lifestyle finds its only valid basis in the message of the cross. Hence, the Christian lifestyle, by its very nature, risks the disapproval and even hatred of the world in order to be true to the message of the cross and in order to communicate the good news of salvation.

Jesus came preaching the good news of the kingdom of God (Mark 1:14-15). Yet, the night Jesus was arrested He told His disciples, "If the world hates you, keep in mind that it hated me first. If you belonged to the world, it would love you as its own. As it is, you do not belong to the world, but I have chosen you out of the world. That is why the world hates you. Remember what I told you: 'A servant is not greater than his master.' If they persecuted me, they will persecute you also. If they obeyed my teaching, they will obey yours also. They will treat you this way because of my name, for they do not know the one who sent me. If I had not come and spoken to them, they would not be guilty of sin; but now they have no excuse for their sin" (John 15:18-22).

Christians should be loving, caring, and tactful. But in our attempt to avoid the offense of the cross, we often fail to be the light of the world that exposes spiritual darkness with the message of God. How can we convince someone they need a Savior if we will not talk about sin? And how can we be followers of God's Word if we do not portray sin biblically? Consider Jesus, who was sent to demonstrate visibly the great love of God, yet He could not avoid the displeasure, even hatred, of men if He was going to convince them of their need for salvation from their sins.

Is it our place to tell people about their sins? Yes. How else can we share the good news of forgiveness from sin? What does it mean to tell people about Jesus, except to say that He loved them so much that He died for their sins? (Of course, no one is qualified to share with someone their need for salvation unless he or she has accepted Christ as Savior and is living a life worthy of the gospel.)

What about Jesus' teaching that we should not judge (Matthew 7:1-5)? There are two important things to understand regarding this. First, the kind of judgment Jesus forbade was the attitude of consigning someone to hell with such finality that we rule out the possibility of their salvation. No human being knows the full course of someone's life. We are meant to witness to every person until the day they are beyond our reach, and not assume (or even hope) for judgment on anyone. We should love and witness to them always. Second, if we are only speaking what the Word of God says, then it is not our personal judgment we are issuing. The judgment is that of the Word of God, which we are relaying to a person. The gospel, the message of the cross, both condemns sin and offers salvation. It is impossible to share only the latter aspect without doing damage to the message.

In John 15 (quoted above), Jesus spoke of the hatred the world had expressed toward Him, its Savior. The only way He could have avoided that hatred would have been to compromise His message, purpose, and ministry. This is exactly the case with His followers.

We make much of religious freedom in America. Our society is pluralistic even in matters of religion. Our nation has historically tolerated a variety of religions, and the freedom of religion is guaranteed by the Constitution. That is good. But let us think in kingdom of God terms, not just social terms. Is the fact that Christianity is "tolerated" a compliment in our favor? It might be noted that wherever the church is most active and vocal on behalf of biblical truth, toleration for the church decreases. Our nation needs to be called to repentance from sin. When the church issues that call, it will receive opposition. This is not to say that Christianity must be hated to be real, for there will be those who are open to the message. But real Christianity will invoke opposition from those determined to defend their sins. (It should be added that where the church declares the gospel faithfully, God's power manifests itself in confirmation. See Mark 16:20 and Acts 14:3.)

We have been conditioned to think that no one has the right to impose their beliefs on others. There is an element of truth to that; we respect the freedom of choice God has given to everyone. But verbally declaring the need for salvation is intrinsic to the lifestyle of a disciple of Christ. It is part of the Christian faith. It is the charge of our Lord. While our nation may be pluralistic, Christianity is exclusivist and evangelistic. It declares that there is only one way to salvation, and that is through Jesus Christ. If we really believe in the love and the judgment of God, in heaven and hell, in good and evil, if we really believe what our faith teaches about these things, then our convictions will necessarily lead us to speak to others about Christ. We will not be satisfied to give a little witness, and then merely say to ourselves that we have done our job and it's up to the other person to decide what to do. The prophets, apostles, and Christian witnesses in the Bible *persuaded* others with urgency, tears, pleading, arguments, and persistency. Their hearts' desire was to convince people with all their might that they needed Jesus. If we think that this will not fit our modern setting, it is easy for us to reinvent discipleship so it is more agreeable to us and our world. But spiritual truth has not changed and eternal souls are still at stake. If we really obeyed God and let His holy light shine into every dark and sinful corner, we would not only be disliked by some, but we would also see many others come to salvation—and that is worth it. In that occupation, many Christians would find again the joy of their own salvation!

Many Christians are attempting to make their impact on society through social activism and legislative action. While involvement in these areas may have their place, the most effective way God has given to us for changing the world is to change one heart at a time with the pure message of the gospel. That message confronts people with the claims of Jesus Christ on their lives.

Peace talks, military strength, arms treaties, diplomacy, economic strategies, political agendas, and picket lines are not the forces of change the world most needs. What is needed most is the gospel presented by God's ambassadors in the world (2 Corinthians 5:16-21). The time and energy of Christ's disciples are best spent in the simple and wholehearted declaration of the message of the cross to people on a personal level.

Christians must live consistently with the claims of the gospel. This is a necessary ingredient for the church's effectiveness in the world. This is *the lifestyle of the cross*. It is the life that is guided by the standards of the teachings of Jesus Christ. It is the life that refuses to compromise those standards in order to be more acceptable to the world and its standards (including some of its religious standards). It is the life that is lived openly before all for God. Such a life is pleasing to God and carries the integrity and authority to share the gospel and convince others of their need to follow Jesus as well. It is the life that demonstrates congruity with the gospel of Jesus Christ.

The lifestyle of the cross is the only option for the disciples of Christ. Christ gave the only criteria acceptable in His sight for discipleship. His teachings about cross-bearing and self-denial are clearly set forth by Jesus as essential to following Him. To reject His terms of discipleship in favor of ours is to live a religious life that is not discipleship as Christ Himself defines and recognizes it. It is a kind of Christianity of our own invention. That life will be lacking in the presence and power of Christ.

The purpose of this book is to discover what Jesus meant when He said that His followers must deny themselves, lose their lives for His sake, and bear their cross. This will involve an exploration of passages in the Bible that teach the message on which the lifestyle of the cross is based and the implications of living that message. Lest the reader think that this will be a book about negatives, let him or her be assured that the lifestyle of the cross is set forth in the Bible as the only way to life in resurrection power now and glory in eternity. It is the path that leads to the experience of the joy of salvation.

The Christian hope makes believers to be optimists in the best sense of the word. The lifestyle of the cross is not a life in which we *seek* self-fulfillment by pleasing ourselves, but rather it is a life in which we trust that joy and peace will *come to* us through complete obedience to God on His terms. In surrendering one's life to God's purpose, the believer knows that it is God's plan to bless. God's purpose in the world is to use believers to bring others to faith. Sometimes God leads His disciples into risky situations in which we must implicitly trust Him.

Jesus is the standard for Christian living and purpose. By worldly standards He was not a "success," nor was He "prosperous" by some religious standards. He would not completely live up to the success and prosperity gospels of today. He was unpopular with the leaders of the people. His circle of friends were common men. He went against the grain of the religious authorities of His day. He owned no permanent residence. He was branded a heretic and a criminal. He was tortured and executed by the authorities. But this was the way to the resurrection. Paul knew that principle when he wrote in Philippians 3:10-11, "I want to know Christ—yes, to know the power of his resurrection and participation in his sufferings, becoming like him in his death, and so, somehow, attaining to the resurrection from the dead." Suffering and resurrection power are joined in one event, and in our truly Christian experience.

Only by living the lifestyle of the cross can we find the power for victorious living, and the power to take the kingdom of darkness by storm!

Chapter Two

On the Way to the Cross

When we consider the singular and distinctive lifestyle, which is herein termed "the lifestyle of the cross," we must, of course, begin with a consideration of the meaning of the cross of Christ. The Christian life is defined by the work of Christ on the cross, and is lived by the very power of the resurrected Christ, a power that is demonstrated in the life of the believer on a daily basis.

The Christian lifestyle can be validly called "the lifestyle of the cross" because, just as it is impossible to take the cross out of Christianity as a belief system and still retain true Christianity, so we cannot take the cross out of our Christian lives and live as genuine Christians. It is my hope that this will become increasingly clear as the reader studies the pages of this book and that the reader will find laid on his or her heart a sense of urgency that will lead him or her to a commitment to the Christ-like life outlined in these chapters.

The cross has become the chief Christian symbol. We place it in our churches, on our pulpits, on our steeples, and wear it as jewelry. Since the early centuries of the Christian church, the cross has been loved and revered and taken as the most appropriate symbol of our faith. Unfortunately, many who wanted to portray themselves and their doctrinal systems and causes as being Christian have also made use of the cross as a symbol.

There is nothing magical about the symbol of the cross. It will not, as some have claimed, protect you from harm or ward off evil spirits if you wear it or hide it under your pillow. In fact, let the reader understand that when I write of the lifestyle of the cross, I am not really referring to the cross as a mere symbol, a symbol that may be and has been used in so many incongruous ways. Rather, I am referring to the actual, historical work of Christ, which has led many to use the symbol of the cross as a point of reference in thinking about that work. On the cross Jesus provided a redemptive sacrifice for all sins, and in speaking of the lifestyle of the cross I am referring to the actual effect that sacrifice has on our lives, and I am referring to the peculiar definition it gives to the life of the true believer.

To speak of the cross is one of the most unlikely ways to represent a movement in a world that promises joy, peace, and happiness. The cross has always represented the worst, most shameful, horrible kind of death. Thus it has been easy for the "positive thinkers" to omit its full implication from their teachings, leaving their hearers with a rather superficial version of its meaning for them.

Yes, the cross represents death and punishment. And it is in that meaning that it remains precious to us and impels us to the fullest kind of gratitude for God's grace and obedience to the Father in all things, for it represents the Son of God's suffering for our sins. It is this meaning that leads Paul to exclaim, *"Oh, the unsearchable riches of Christ!"* Only in this fullness of its meaning can we possibly be moved to that same wonder and love for God. For the cross to remain the place where victory was won over human sin, we must never try to remove the meaning of suffering and death from it.

The cross as a form of punishment did not come into use only in Jesus' time. It had been a form of execution long before. The Persians invented it to keep prisoners from dying on the ground, which they considered to be sacred. The Phoenicians used it to prolong the suffering of criminals. Later, the Romans adopted crucifixion as a means to punish and deter crime and they became more efficient at it than any before them. There was nothing unique about the cross as a means of punishment. Many common criminals had died this slow, suffocating death. Thousands at a time had been crucified by the Romans. It was the most feared of all forms of punishment. It was renowned as a symbol of pain, death, and oppression.

Yet, the cross became the most beloved of symbols for Christians. It represents suffering, but also victory for the believer, for Jesus' death on the cross for us was not a permanent death. He rose from the dead bodily on the third day. Thus, the cross represents not only death, but also the overcoming power of divine life on our behalf. Atonement was won through Christ's death, and its benefits are ever available to each person through His life now and forever, for it was our death penalty Jesus took on Himself, our sins He atoned for. The fact that the cross is so loved, and became so loved even during the time when crucifixion was still practiced, is one of the greatest proofs that Jesus did indeed rise from the dead. The cross once meant death alone, but it was transformed into a banner of victory, even at a time when men were still dying upon it. In the same way, to trust in Jesus' work on the cross is to find your life of testing and trials transformed into something meaningful. The Christian life is a life changed from the spiritual death from which you could not rescue yourself, to resurrection life from God.

Now, it is true that the cross represents victory over sin, but it also represents suffering. That meaning was not taken away when Jesus rose from the dead. That meaning has never been removed. The cross represents God's love and redemptive plan, a plan that was accomplished through suffering. Jesus rose and lives, but still we cannot deny the cross its full meaning; the cross will not relinquish that meaning. And so, as we talk about abundant and victorious living, we will also see that we cannot escape the quality of sacrifice found in true Christian living with a redemptive purpose in a sinful world. It is the *purpose* of the Christian's life in the world that brings about the element of *risk,* and so to avoid the risk is to bypass the purpose of witness to sinners.

The message of the cross was never a sad or negative one for the first Christians. They gloried in it. They rejoiced in it, even in the midst of suffering. They were so in love with the One who died for them that the suffering they endured for His name was considered entirely worthwhile. They were not lovers of pain, but they loved God and knew the only meaning their lives could have was in Him. If sinners, out of hatred for God or the message of salvation from sin, inflicted pain on them, the disciples of Christ remained undaunted.

Today, our hope lies in the cross. We must not try to change it. Our very lives depend on the reality of the sacrifice of Jesus. The cross is a source of rejoicing. Coupled with the historical truth of the bodily resurrection of Christ, it embodies all of the meaning of life, for "eternal life" in the Bible has not only to do with quantity, but also quality and purpose. God, being the only Eternal One, the sole possessor of eternal life, shares His life with us. That is what it means to have eternal life. God's life is not only everlasting; it is a certain *kind* of life—holy, loving, purposeful. Receiving eternal life, then, brings about a radical change of life because we share God's quality of life.

Christ lived the lifestyle of the cross in its ultimate expression so that we might live eternally. And even though we receive abundant life from the living Lord, still we cannot remove any of the meaning of the cross without leaving ourselves bereft of the vital meaning of Christian living. God is the source of our comfort and happiness. The lifestyle of the cross is an abundant and positive life. Yet it is impossible to remove the aspect of sacrifice from the Christian life without ignoring a significant aspect of the meaning of the cross.

Let us make the cross of Christ our starting point from which we will develop our understanding of what the basis of Christian living and discipleship really is. Matthew 20:17-19 says, "Now Jesus was going up to Jerusalem. On the way, he took the twelve aside and said to them, 'We are going up to Jerusalem, and the Son of Man will be delivered over to the chief priests and the teachers of the law. They will condemn him to death and will hand him over to the Gentiles to be mocked and flogged and crucified. On the third day he will be raised to life!'"

As we read this passage we find Jesus on His way to Jerusalem. He is on His way to the cross. He has predicted to His disciples several times that certain things were going to happen when He arrived at Jerusalem. In Matthew 16:21 He said that He would suffer many things and be killed. In Matthew 17:22-23 Jesus said again that He would be killed. Here, in Matthew 20, He is even more detailed in His prediction: He would be mocked, scourged, and crucified at the hands of the Gentiles, having been handed over to them by the Jews.

Jesus saw clearly what lay before Him. He knew He would suffer and die. Already, as He walked toward the cross, He began to feel its terrible weight on His shoulders, for the cross was more than a piece of wood; it represented that event at which the weight of the whole world's sin would be laid on Him. Is it any wonder that He was in such agony in Gethsemane that He declared that His soul was sorrowful even unto death? Imagine the weight of all sin and guilt being borne by one man, and a man who had never known sin! Imagine the stress as He prepared to take upon Himself all the physical, spiritual, mental, and emotional problems of mankind—the results of sin and death coming into the world—by way of a tortuous ordeal that by itself would cause anyone to shrink back!

Jesus knew that it was for this that He was born. The weight of the anticipated cross grew as the time drew nearer; grew until He would eventually cry tears and sweat blood in anguished prayer; grew as He faced accusers and torturers, knowing there was more suffering to come; grew until finally He was nailed cruelly to that cross to bear in love the penalty of all sin. Our sin!

What sort of suffering must Jesus endure?

BETRAYAL

Jesus suffered abandonment by friends and the failure of other people. This alone is heartbreaking enough and has brought many down. But to make matters worse, He also suffered outright betrayal by one friend. And He suffered denial on the part of another friend. In His time of greatest need, those who claimed the greatest love for Him left Him alone, driven by fear and the impulse of self-preservation. Jesus said that the greatest love is demonstrated when a man lays down his life for a friend. He was speaking primarily of Himself, but now, at His time of trial, His closest friends protected themselves.

CONDEMNED TO DEATH

Jesus suffered the ultimate injustice. He had sinned no sin, done no wrong. He was framed by those who were jealous of Him, those who could not abide His words of truth and holiness of life. But He endured it willingly for our sakes. He suffered *injustice* so we would not be doomed without remedy to receive the *just* penalty of our sins. He brought us the grace and mercy of God.

Injustice is very hard to bear. We want to defend ourselves from injustice. To imagine that we may be falsely accused and wrongly condemned and sentenced is a nightmare thought of hopelessness and helplessness. Yet Jesus was in no way helpless. He surrendered His life. He laid it down. It was not taken from Him. He willingly bore all this for us. (See John 10:11-18; 18:7-11; Matthew 26:50-54.)

It is ironic that people can be so angered by blatant injustices (murder, terrorism, innocent victims of war), and outraged at personal insults, and yet be so unmoved that a sinless man died to pay the penalty of their own sins.

MOCKED

Jesus suffered humiliation. The soldiers made sport of Him, insulted Him, and handled Him roughly. They spit on Him, struck Him in the face, pulled His beard out, and laughed at Him.

Have we ever been insulted as greatly as Christ? Have we ever borne rejection as He did in order to fulfill His mission of dying for our sins? This was the Son of God! Would we even think of allowing such a thing to happen to us, if we had the status and power to prevent it?

Let us never be afraid or feel self-pity when we are mocked because of our faith. Remember Jesus, who suffered insult, injury, spittle, beating, laughter, and danger for us because He loves us. There is nothing ignominious about suffering for Him. We who love Jesus must never fear the indignities and abuses of unbelievers when we live and act and speak in Jesus' name. And while we wish to be winsome and attract people to Jesus, let us never apologize for the offense of the gospel, nor try to restate it in a way more acceptable to the world at the cost of its true insistence that sin be forsaken. Let us endure for Christ's sake!

Romans 15:3 says, "For even Christ did not please himself but, as it is written: 'The insults of those who insult you have fallen on me.'" And 1 Peter 2:21-24 says, "To this you were called, because Christ suffered for you, leaving you an example, that you should follow in his steps. 'He committed no sin, and no deceit was found in his mouth.' When they hurled their insults at him, he did not retaliate; when he suffered, he made no threats. Instead, he entrusted himself to him who judges justly. 'He himself bore our sins' in his body on the cross, so that we might die to sins and live for righteousness; 'by his wounds you have been healed.'"

Defensive Christians react differently than Christ did, and so fail to demonstrate the lifestyle of the cross. 1 Peter 4:14 says, "If you are insulted because of the name of Christ, you are blessed, for the Spirit of glory and of God rests on you."

SCOURGED

Jesus suffered physical attack and pain. The Jews practiced whipping using leather thongs only. The law forbade lashing a criminal more than forty times, so they limited it to thirty-nine strokes, lest a possible miscount would cause them to unwittingly violate the law. Additionally, the Jews limited the range of the lashing to the back of the prisoner.

However, Jesus was scourged by the Romans. The Roman scourge consisted of several leather thongs embedded with bits of metal, stone, or shell. The use of such an instrument literally pounded the victim's back to raw meat, and then shredded the flesh away in ribbons. There were no limitations as to where on the victim's body the scourge could be laid. Often the prisoner was scourged the entire length of his body. Additionally, there was no limitation as to the number of lashes that could be inflicted. There was usually a soldier watching the punishment whose task it was to call a halt to the scourging before the prisoner died. The purpose of this was to prolong the suffering from the wounds received. Sometimes the victim died anyway from blood loss and shock. The Roman scourge was so feared that it was called "the second death." It was usually considered sufficient punishment by itself, and rarely was a prisoner both scourged and crucified.

Who among Jesus' followers has been asked to suffer such pain lately? True, many have suffered. Many are suffering. But in the United States, it is generally true that believers expect to live their Christian faith without full-scale persecution. We expect ideological opposition, but not real persecution.

How many of us balk at the inconveniences we are sometimes called upon to endure just to get to church, be involved, and share the gospel? Will we willingly suffer for the Savior?

CRUCIFIED

Jesus suffered death itself. He gathered upon Himself all the sins of the world and the consequences thereof, and then He died. It was no ordinary death. It was our death. It was the death of the innocent for the guilty in order to make the guilty innocent.

Jesus walked to the cross, taking the task God the Father assigned to Him, taking the road appointed Him. All who wish to follow His example must be willing to count the cost (Luke 14:25-33). The price for our atonement is paid in full. But wholehearted service to God takes complete obedience, not just partial obedience. We cannot obey God only insofar as it is convenient, or insofar as it does not interfere with our other involvements, or insofar as it makes us feel good, or insofar as it does not offend others. While we are on this earth we have a joyous, but serious, task to fulfill for the sake of other souls. Jesus taught us this by His own example. If any think it is otherwise, it is because they have not counted the cost. Indeed, many rebel at the very idea that the Christian life might include a cost, and are attracted instead to teachers who say that material prosperity, and possibly social influence, will be the result and evidence of their faith. They like the idea that real Christians won't have anything to worry about in terms of health and finances. They spend their days trying to conform to such a gospel, and feeling guilty when bad things happen, obviously revealing a flaw in their faith and spirituality. We are very caught up these days with what God will do for us, but we consider very little about what God wants us to do for Him, or about the cost of discipleship Jesus spoke about.

Jesus knew that it would cost Him everything to redeem and rescue us. He willingly paid that price so that we would never have to pay it. That price was His own blood—praise be to God! What, then, shall be the sort of commitment we give in return? The only acceptable answer is: commitment to the person of our Lord and to His redemptive purpose in the world.

Of what sort is our love, gratitude, and allegiance? Did not Jesus tell His followers that it was His joy and peace and comfort He would leave them in a world filled with sadness, turmoil, and strife? Did He not pray that our joy might be full? Did He not say that He had overcome the world? Did He not promise the Comforter, the Holy Spirit? Joy, peace, comfort, salvation, eternal life—what gifts! What cause for rejoicing! He gave them to us, but He paid for them with His own blood!

What a price He paid! The anguished prayers, the forsakenness, the cruelty, the torture, the cross. Six long hours on the cross. What person reading this has been asked to do that? But Jesus did it. And if we suffer, it is no longer for *our* sins, but for love of our Lord and total dedication and obedience to Him in a sinful and violent world, in the hope that we might save some.

If we could look backward in time and catch a glimpse of the Son of God suffering on the cross, who could behold such a sight! Let us pray for such a moving vision. The cross reveals God's will, God's love. Such a picture glimpsed with our spiritual eyes is what will compel us to commit ourselves to being what God wants us to be.

We have been bought with a great price. Do we always live as though our life—heart, mind, body, and soul—belongs exclusively to God? Do we always live as though someone really died for us personally? Do we feel compelled to take the message of the cross to those bound by sin, to those who are addicted, alone, imprisoned, poverty-stricken, bitter, troubled—all those for whom Christ died? Does our love for Jesus, our love for lost souls, and the importance of the message send us forth with urgency?

Remember, salvation is free. Christian living involves a cross. Jesus paid His price of obedience. Will you do the same for the love of Him? Certainly, our salvation is by grace through faith and not by works. But love, for each other and for Christ, is not a matter of words only, but of action and obedience.

RESURRECTION

Of course, the cross event includes the resurrection of Christ. Without that His death would have been in vain. But the way to that victory involved the cross. And so it always remains, as will be demonstrated in the pages ahead. The Bible promises eternal glory to those willing to identify their lives with the cross of Christ and so commit themselves to God's will that they will be willing to risk rejection and suffering to do it.

Psalm 116:12-14 says it well: "What shall I return to the LORD for all his goodness to me? I will lift up the cup of salvation and call on the name of the LORD. I will fulfill my vows to the LORD in the presence of all his people."

Chapter Three

Bearing the Cross

All who call themselves Christians are claiming to be followers of Jesus Christ. But if we are going to make such an important claim, then it behooves us to understand accurately what that means. The first question that must be asked is, who decides what it means to be a follower of Jesus Christ? Who sets the standard? Who sets forth the definition of what a Christian is? Is it up to each individual believer? Does this conclusion rest with some church council?

Let us insist on the premise that the only person who can define what it means to follow Christ is Jesus Christ Himself! This means that we must consult His teachings and find out how He defines Christian discipleship in order to be able to make a decision to follow Christ according to His expectations. We must be disciples on His terms, not our own, for if we decide to be Christians on our own terms, we risk not being followers of Christ in His eyes. Jesus plainly declared that many would call Him "Lord," but He would disown them if they did not do what He said (Matthew 7:21-23; Luke 6:46).

Jesus Himself set forth His terms (and thus the only valid terms) of discipleship in Matthew 16:24-25: "Then Jesus said to his disciples, 'Whoever wants to be my disciple must deny themselves and take up their cross and follow me. For whoever wants to save their life will lose it, but whoever loses their life for me will find it.'" (Read also Matthew 10:38; Luke 14:27; 9:23-24.)

This passage of Scripture describes the conditions of following Jesus as set forth by Jesus Himself. Using the above text in Matthew 16 as our starting point, let us consider the true Christian life in terms of self-denial and cross-bearing, since these are two of the distinctive characteristics of discipleship that Jesus mandates.

"Whoever wants to be my disciple must . . . follow me."

To come after, or follow, means to adhere and remain close to someone. Here it means to keep Jesus Christ before you as the standard, pattern, and example that will determine the direction and shape of your life. To follow Jesus means that the teachings of Jesus are held by you to be supremely authoritative in all you believe and do. This requires conviction on your part regarding who Jesus is, a genuine love for Him, a devoted commitment to Him, a faith in His work on the cross on your behalf, and a stubborn decision to obey Him. To follow Jesus means that you follow closely in His footsteps, no matter what it requires of you. 1 Peter 2:21 says, "To this you were called, because Christ suffered for you, leaving you an example, that you should follow in his steps."

As a teenager, I once heard my pastor, E.B. Jones, say that Jesus has many admirers, but not enough followers. That statement stuck in my mind. There are many who attend church weekly, but their professions of Christianity may be lived out superficially, or at any rate, at their convenience. Following Jesus is not merely acknowledging His existence, or "agreeing" with His teachings. Following Jesus means to walk in His footsteps. It means to take upon yourself His purpose and mission in the world. It means seeking to reconcile people with God. It means braving the dangers of an evil world for the sake of an unbendable love for God and for people. It is doing what Christ did and letting Him live His divine and redemptive life through us.

Jesus calls us to a determined identification of ourselves with Him in every part of our lives. What does that mean? Each chapter of this book will treat some aspect of this kind of discipleship, which is herein termed "the lifestyle of the cross." It should be kept in mind that this volume does not claim to be an exhaustive treatment, for there is something more to learn every day.

What was the occasion for the words of Jesus in Matthew 16? Jesus had just predicted His immanent death and Peter was in a state of confusion at hearing this prediction. Peter believed that Jesus was the long-awaited Messiah. Therefore, he believed in the truthfulness of Jesus' words. But Jesus' prediction of His own death at the hands of sinners was in direct contradiction to the messianic expectations of that day, which Peter had been taught. Death at the hands of sinners was not to be the destiny of the Messiah of God. Contemporary teachings held that the Messiah could not die. Add to this Peter's love for and devotion to Jesus, and we can easily understand how it came to be that Peter, in his startled disbelief, was so bold and desperate as to rebuke the One he had just called the Son of the living God.

Jesus in turn rebuked Peter, calling him His adversary (the meaning of the Greek word *satanos*, usually translated "Satan") for troubling Him at a time when He was preparing for the coming ordeal. He declared to Peter that he was putting the concerns of men (the messianic expectations and desires of the time) above God's actual will and plan (which was for the Messiah to suffer for the sins of the whole world).

Peter had not yet come to understand the meaning Christ would give to the hated executioner's cross. In the meantime,

Jesus declared that willingness to enter into partnership with Him in the suffering of the cross is a condition of following Him. He will accept no other kind of followship.

Elsewhere, Jesus declared that willingness to suffer as manifest evidence of His own love for the Father. In John 14:29-31, He said, "I have told you now before it happens, so that when it does happen you will believe. I will not say much more to you, for the prince of this world is coming. He has no hold over me, but he comes so that the world may learn that I love the Father and do exactly what my Father has commanded me."

In our text in Matthew 16, Jesus makes the willingness to give oneself completely out of love for the Lord a test and standard of true discipleship. When Jesus told His disciples that they must deny themselves, lose their lives in their love for Him, and take up their cross and bear it, He was saying to His followers, in effect, "I am so committed to the Father and to you that I will go to the cross. If you want to be my disciple, you must be just that committed to me. Your whole life must be mine. Your whole obedience must be to Me."

I once saw a poster of Christ on the cross. The caption declared, "Jesus said, 'I love you this much,' then He stretched out His arms and died." So Jesus tells us that it is impossible to be His disciple unless we, too, are willing to bear the cross of redemption to the world in His name and in complete love for Him—whatever the cost. We must share the work He did on Calvary with everyone we can. This involves total commitment and sacrifice on our parts.

"Take up [your] cross..."

When Jesus made mention of the cross, pictures of shame, oppression, pain, suffering, injustice, and death immediately leapt to the minds of the disciples. As yet, this was their only frame of reference regarding the cross. Only after the resurrection of Jesus would the elements of salvation, victory, and eternal life be added to that picture.

To those of us who know the whole picture, the cross must still retain all of its original meanings of suffering and sacrifice. Only then can it also stand for unconditional love and grace. We must not reject the meanings of suffering and sacrifice, but we must rather include them with the more positive meanings of redemptive love, divine reconciliation, and victory over sin and death. All of these are necessary to the complete portrayal of the cross of Christ, then and now.

Peter, Paul, and indeed all the apostles and New Testament writers, taught and lived out all of these meanings of crossbearing. They did not only choose to regard those meanings that were convenient to the flesh and attractive to the world. While they spoke about and experienced love, joy, peace, and abundant life, they also willingly experienced the persecution and hardship that remained part of the meaning of the cross of Christ. Thus, they bore the cross and fulfilled their discipleship. They did not suffer from a desire for martyrdom, but they had a complete and obedient love for their Lord.

When many think of cross-bearing, they think of putting up with human weaknesses. But the Bible is teaching something much more than merely an attitude of resignation to human frailties (which all too often leads to excusing ourselves from being all that God has made it possible for us to be in Christ). Instead, the Bible is speaking of the complete and loving identification of our lives with Christ, what He stands for, and what He wants to accomplish through us in this dark world. The gospel of health, wealth, and prosperity may attract some people by appealing to their desire for pleasure, comfort, and success, but it will not convict them of their sins. If you begin to speak to such people (for their sakes) about their sins (for which Christ died) you may be rejected, but you may also save some.

If Jesus is our Lord and Example, then we as Christians find the meaning of *our* cross in what the cross meant *for Christ*. To bear our cross in devotion to Christ means to identify ourselves with what He did for us, to identify our lives completely with His redemptive work on the cross, even to the point, if necessary, of suffering for that identification as we live joyous but uncompromisingly holy lives and actively share the gospel with others. Thus, the pattern of the true Christian life is Jesus Christ, in both His redemptive suffering in and for an evil world, and His victory over death and sin in His resurrection.

The lifestyle of the cross is victory through commitment that may bring pain. It is joy through love that may bring suffering. It is a combination of laying down our lives for a purpose, and living our lives in glorious victory over all the bondage of sin. Jesus is both the Suffering Servant and the King of kings, and the true children of God bear both aspects of Christ's image in their character, in their daily living, and in the meaning they find in life.

We cannot deviate from applying all of the meanings of the cross to our own Christian lives if we are to be disciples by Jesus' definition. That application must be made not only theologically, but practically as well. The Christian life is indeed characterized by joy, peace, and power. But it is also a life of mission, God's mission, in a sinful world. Therein do we find our purpose for existing in the world. As such, we may suffer awhile until our own individual part in that mission is ended and God takes us home. But we can say with Paul, "I consider that our present sufferings are not worth comparing with the glory that will be revealed in us" (Romans 8:18). We must be willing to spend ourselves in the often risky business of doing the Father's will in this kind of world. We cannot choose to suit ourselves as to which parts of God's will appeal to us and which parts do not. The underlying premise of calling sinners away from sin to holy living is that God's will is permanent. And that premise will always call forth negative responses from a world that resists the truth we confess and the conviction of sin's wickedness, which conviction our lives may cause.

We, as Christians, must receive all the life God calls us into— abundance and blessing, obedience and sacrifice. This is not to suggest anything like a doctrine of salvation by works. But the one who has already been saved by grace through faith ought to go on to the quality, style, and motivation of the lifestyle of the cross that Jesus pronounced to be the only true evidence of discipleship. (One might call it "works *because of* salvation," for while we do not do good works to be saved, being saved should naturally lead to doing good works; otherwise, one's salvation is in question, there being no evidence of it.) God is the God of all comfort (2 Corinthians 1:3-4), but Christianity is not an easy-chair religion or Sunday morning habit (2 Corinthians 1:5). It is powerful and effective cross-bearing for the love of God to bring the message of the crucified and living One to a needy world. The lifestyle of the cross is a Christian walk that is redemptive in its every aspect. In our short time on this earth, we must prepare ourselves and others for eternity.

Karl Marx said that religion is the opium of the people. By that definition, *biblical* Christianity could not be a religion, for *biblical* Christianity certainly does not allow for a protected, unopposed existence. It is not a mere crutch to make believers cope with life. Instead, Acts 14:22 says of Paul and Barnabas that in the course of "strengthening the disciples and encouraging them to remain true to the faith," they said to them, "We must go through many hardships to enter the kingdom of God."

"deny themselves . . . loses their life"

When Jesus said this, He wasn't speaking of mere pious asceticism. When properly understood, Jesus is speaking of practical and essential terms of true discipleship.

What does it mean to deny yourself? It is not a matter of denying yourself *things*, but denying your *self*. It means that you lose sight of your selfish interests in giving preference to the interests of Christ. Christ and His will become the central focus of your life. You don't build your life on your willfulness, as moral, religious, and sensible as it may appear to be. Rather, you seek with all your heart to know what pleases God. You recognize that this knowledge cannot be based merely on your own opinion, but on the Word of God and the voice of His Spirit as you carefully attend daily to your relationship with God.

This does not mean that you are left without exercise of will and choice. These are important human and spiritual qualities that God has given to us, without which we could not choose to come into a relationship with Him when He drew us, and without which we cannot act determinedly in obedience to Him when we understand His will. Rather, denying yourself means that your will conforms to God's will by your choice and surrender (having first recognized His call and claim on your life). As you grow in fellowship and relationship with God, and seek to understand His will, you willingly choose His will for your life. You allow His will to change you, challenge you, form your values and purpose in life. This is the difference between selfish *willfulness* on the one hand, and committed *willingness* on the other. Both involve your will, in exactly opposite ways.

This is as it was always meant to be. The person dominated by his or her selfish will has deviated from the purpose of God's created humanity (and this includes the religious person who, notwithstanding her religiousness, is not doing God's will).

Thinking themselves to be free because they are going their own way, those who seek their own way become more bound to sin as they move further from God and His good will for them.

Genesis 1:26-27 says, "Then God said, 'Let us make mankind in our image, in our likeness, so that they may rule over the fish in the sea and the birds in the sky, over the livestock and all the wild animals, and over all the creatures that move along the ground.' So God created mankind in his own image, in the image of God he created them; male and female he created them." Speaking of those who now are committed to following Jesus Christ, Colossians 3:9-10 says, "Do not lie to each other, since you have taken off your old self with its practices and have put on the new self, which is being renewed in knowledge in the image of its Creator." Becoming a Christian means to be restored to the relationship with God and the kind of life the Creator intended from the beginning. It means that you find your true identity as a man or woman totally bound up in the cross event. It means enjoying the benefits of Christ's atoning work in full freedom from sin and partnership in the true will and work of God.

The true Christian disciple makes Christ, not self, the center of life in all decisions, attitudes, deeds, relationship, and words. The follower of Jesus does not merely schedule Jesus into his life when he has time between other interests and commitments. Instead, Jesus *is* the disciple's life.

The lifestyle of the cross certainly is not self-centered. It is patterned after the example of Christ, who selflessly laid down His life in love and obedience to the Father. He did this because He loved us and desired to bring about our wholeness. Thus, the life of the genuine follower after Christ is characterized by obedience to God's commands, submission to God's entire will, service to God's purpose, and the sacrificial willingness to risk suffering for God's redemptive plan for the world. The Christian values life in terms of eternity, not mere temporal comfort. All this is motivated by Christ's love for us made known to us and working through us. 2 Corinthians 5:14-15 says, "For Christ's love compels us, because we are convinced that one died for all, and therefore all died. And he died for all, that those who live should no longer live for themselves but for him who died for them and was raised again."

The alternative is to act out our own kind of discipleship, designed to agree with our plans, conceptions, opinions, ambitions, preferences, desires, feelings, values, and our own determination of what should be done. We (and our preferred form of Christianity) become the standard, rather than Christ. Such a "discipleship" will be lived at our convenience, according to our schedule, thus producing a discipleship and ministry that lack the spontaneity we see in Christ's ministry. We will avoid risks, and create a theology and understanding of the church that justify self-preservation and promote pet ideas. We will make the rules of our faith and walk accordingly. And our goal will often be self-fulfillment according to our wants and according to our wisdom regarding what is good for us. Additionally, we will cherish public approval, and lead ourselves to believe that therein lies the proof of our righteousness. Let us listen to the voice of God who says, "Woe to the obstinate children . . . to those who carry out plans that are not mine, forming an alliance, but not by my Spirit, heaping sin upon sin" (Isaiah 30:1).

Remember, the cross of Christ is our standard. Philippians 2:5-8 says, "In your relationships with one another, have the same mindset as Christ Jesus: Who, being in very nature God, did not consider equality with God something to be used to his own advantage; rather, he made himself nothing by taking the very nature of a servant, being made in human likeness. And being found in appearance as a man, he humbled himself by becoming obedient to death—even death on a cross!"

In true Christian living we no longer place our self at the heart of all we do. We trust God to bring about our well-being as we seek first His kingdom and righteousness, and go on in submission to what He has revealed to us of His plans and ways. God's ways are not always the course we would have followed aided only by our own reasoning powers. But God's ways are infinitely superior. Only human arrogance can argue otherwise. "'For my thoughts are not your thoughts, neither are your ways my ways,' declares the LORD. 'As the heavens are higher than the earth, so are my ways higher than your ways and my thoughts than your thoughts'" (Isaiah 55:8-9).

Thus, to deny yourself means to recognize God's authority and lordship. We do not try to assert our will on God, but surrender to His will. To deny yourself means to dethrone your self from rule over your life, and to enthrone God as King over everything. And it means to do it joyfully and trustingly. Every decision, every action, every thought, every word is to be fully dedicated to God's will, allowing no one and nothing else to be your master. This is not self-extinction; rather, in self-surrender one finds the real joy and fulfillment that comes not by human but by divine blessing. If you want to achieve your own blessing, you have only done what you can humanly do and have robbed yourself of the power of God's blessing. But God can bless in ways we cannot bless ourselves. God wants each of us to be free from selfishness and futility. To do this we must give up our own faulty will for our lives and seek the will of the One who is never selfish, never frustrated by failure, and who has infinite wisdom and power to share with us.

Colossians 3:1-5 says, "Since, then, you have been raised with Christ, set your hearts on things above, where Christ is, seated at the right hand of God. Set your minds on things above, not on earthly things. For you died, and your life is now hidden with Christ in God. When Christ, who is your life, appears, then you also will appear with him in glory. Put to death, therefore, whatever belongs to your earthly nature." By receiving from God forgiveness and purification from sins, and by surrendering our lives to Him totally, we discover that we are free from the old selfish nature. We need no longer be limited by sin and the weakness of the old flesh. Rather than being earthbound, our lives are truly situated in heaven in Christ. And because our lives are hidden with Christ in heaven, we can forsake the need to preserve ourselves from the consequences of serving Him in this sinful world.

All of this is true when your life is all about Jesus Christ. He bought you. You owe your life to Him. What Jesus did for you provides you with your sole direction and motivation in all you do and say.

Luke 9:23 says that we must deny ourselves "daily." Following Jesus requires daily, consistent living in a surrendered state—not repeated surrenders and "recommitments," but an ongoing condition of surrender and commitment. This means daily living the lifestyle of the cross, daily having the attitude of Jesus. To try to retain willful control of our lives in any aspect is to cast aside the cross and the meaning of cross-bearing, and it is to refuse Jesus' lordship and terms of discipleship.

Chapter Four

The Message of the Cross

We have already noted that the cross of Christ is the sole basis of the Christian life. This includes attitudes, relationships, decisions, goals, etc. Let me reiterate at this point that, in speaking of the cross, I am thinking of both the crucifixion and resurrection of Jesus as constituting one "cross event." The cross of Christ, or the "cross event," is the only basis of a true Christian experience, from beginning to end. Christ's life and work define the true Christian life. This being so, it was necessary to begin our study by considering the meanings of the cross for Christ, and in doing so to discover its meaning for us. We have discovered those meanings to be a marvelous mixture of suffering, despisement, endurance, obedience, and victory.

In the meanings of the cross event we discover the meaning of genuine discipleship. And the essential Christian message is perceived and declared as *the message of the cross*. This message completely informs our spiritual walk, the "lifestyle of the cross." 1 Corinthians 2:1-5 says, "When I came to you, I did not come with eloquence or human wisdom as I proclaimed to you the testimony about God. For I resolved to know nothing while I was with you except Jesus Christ and him crucified. I came to you in weakness with great fear and trembling. My message and my preaching were not with wise and persuasive words, but with a demonstration of the Spirit's power, so that your faith might not rest on human wisdom, but on God's power."

In these words Paul declared that the sole basis of his preaching and lifestyle was the cross of Christ—that is, the redemptive work of Christ, who died and rose from the dead. This was the heart of his message, the lone subject of his preaching. All the wisdom of his message lay in the true portrayal of the cross of Christ, and not in his own ability to reason and argue eloquently. All the strength and effectiveness of his testimony and life lay in the power of the work of Christ in the cross event. Paul admitted his weakness and inadequacy and credited God with any capability he possessed and for every accomplishment. It was not in him but in his message that power resided, and only because it was based on the cross. Such a gospel had inherent power, for it came from God.

It was Paul's decision that his life and message would portray Christ, the crucified One who lives again! In 1 Corinthians 2:2 he wrote, "For I resolved to know nothing while I was with you except Jesus Christ and him crucified." The Greek word for "know" here means "to perceive," "to see," "to know by experience." It is not just intellectual knowledge; rather, it is first-hand, experiential knowledge of Christ that was the focus of Paul's message. Paul was determined to *know* Christ experientially, and to hold nothing else up before people by way of word or deed. His primary desire was that others might *perceive* the Savior. Crucial to his success was a decision to hold nothing before his own eyes, except the Christ who had been crucified as an atonement for his sins.

If we are going to live the lifestyle of the cross and communicate through word and example nothing but the redemptive love of Christ, then we, too, must allow nothing— no self-centeredness, worldliness, or other preoccupation— to distort our vision of the cross, or our portrayal of the cross. We must "know" nothing else but the Christ who was crucified for our sins and who now lives! *That* is the lifestyle of the cross!

The cross event must be ever kept before our eyes as that which guides our thoughts, attitudes, words, and actions. The cross and all that it means (love, suffering, patience, grace, service, reconciliation, the means of overcoming, etc.) must always be our frame of reference—not merely the predominate frame of reference, but the only one. Ask yourself this question: "What affects my life and relationships more than anything else? What, above all, do I consider to be the guide in all my decision-making processes?" Have you ever really thought about it? If you cannot say with definite conviction that the cross and its meanings gives the overriding directives in all your thinking, motives, choices, and actions, your Christian life is badly out of focus. Only a determined refocusing on the cross-bearing life will free your life and witness from those things that hinder and weaken you.

In 1 Corinthians 2:2, the phrase "and him crucified" is in the Greek present tense, which indicates a past action that was completed and has continuing results. The phrase should be literally rendered, "and him *having been* crucified." Jesus is not *still* crucified. That is not our portrayal of Him. The effect of the verse is, "I have decided to know nothing but Christ and the ongoing results of His completed work on the cross." Though the cross event happened long ago, its effects have not diminished in regards to its atoning power. Therefore, the message of the cross contains no loss of the power of God than what it had in Paul's time. It has not become irrelevant in any of its particulars. It is still trustworthy today as a basis of living according to God's will.

Here, then, is the basis of the lifestyle of the cross: it is the message of the cross. And the lifestyle of the cross requires the sharing of the message.

There are two aspects of sharing the message of the cross. The first has to do with the presentation of the message. The second has to do with the demonstration of the message.

THE PRESENTATION OF THE MESSAGE OF THE CROSS

In presenting the gospel, Paul did not lean on his own wisdom or power of debate. He did not try to devise some theology that would be impressive to the scholars and philosophers of his day. He depended not on his powers of persuasion (though he tried to be as persuasive as he could be), nor did he depend on his charismatic personality. Rather, his faith was only in the truth and the power of the message itself when proclaimed. God promised to work through the message. The gospel is the Word of God, and as such it has inherent, divine power. Paul simply preached the cross of Christ, and trusted in the infinite, incomparable wisdom found therein. He did not try to reinvent the gospel, or improve upon it. He shared it as it was.

In 2 Corinthians 10:10, Paul mentioned an opinion some in Corinth had of him as a preacher: "For some say, 'His letters are weighty and forceful, but in person he is unimpressive and his speaking amounts to nothing.'" It appears that not everyone considered Paul to have been a powerful orator by the standards of that day. At that time in Greco-Roman society, more importance was often placed on how eloquently an orator spoke than on the truth of what was said. Technique was more valued than truthfulness of content. By Paul's own admission he preached with fear and trembling, but with a desire to declare the message of the Jesus who loved us and was crucified for our salvation.

We study Paul's message today and recognize the spiritual depth and confidence of the written words. Yet, the power we sense is something beyond the man Paul. The apostle did not depend on his own powers, but rather on the use God would make of his obedience. Paul trusted implicitly in the power God had placed in the message of the cross. This freed him to share the gospel despite his own felt weakness because he trusted that the gospel had a power of its own given to it by God.

Paul wrote to the Corinthian believers that he came to them in "fear and trembling." He came fully conscious of his weakness and inadequacy to accomplish what the gospel accomplishes. But he preached anyway, convinced that a power other than himself was at work whenever he faithfully preached the message. Paul was bold and confident, but not in himself. He didn't stake his effectiveness to his own natural abilities. He spoke mindful of the power of the message entrusted to him and the importance of the task.

Today, the approach to preaching and witnessing is often the opposite. Having little faith in the gospel's own power and undiminished relevance, many preachers and evangelists feel that they must make it more palatable for the modern audience. They declare their sense of confidence in their ability to strengthen the message by their own powers and presentations. Often, the result is that the power of the gospel is diminished by the presumptions and innovations of men.

Do we tremble as we think of the task of sharing the message of the cross? Take heart in the knowledge that you have been entrusted with a great power, which resides in that message, a power to change the hearts of people and give them eternal life! All that is needed from you is your faithful living and sharing of the message of the cross. Any hesitancy on your part is due, at least in part, to an inadequate realization of these things. Feeble though we may we, God made us instruments of HIS gospel, and we will be channels of God's power only to the degree that we obey and share the message of what Christ has done for us. We are called to be "servants of the word" (Luke 1:2).

Every Christian has a trust. This trust is ultimately from God—not from any human source. Our Christian joy is discovered and sustained only when we plunge into the labor of knowing Christ and Him crucified, not only in the context of the church fellowship, but also in the world. That involves not only that we be visible examples, but also that we make a *verbal* declaration of our testimony.

A lost world lies before us! Will you be happy simply paying someone else to carry the message? God has called some to give full time to the ministry of the Word, and He has called the church to support them. But all who have received the free gift of God's grace, the salvation they did not and could not merit by their own works, are now debtors required to share the gospel with all others (Romans 1:14). Sharing the message of the cross is the only proper and adequate response to what God has done for us. Testifying for Christ, in fact, should be the most natural thing in the world for those whose lives have been rescued and changed.

Paul emphasized that he did not come with words merely chosen for the approval of worldly-minded men (or even of many religious thinkers). He was not attempting to induce anyone to believe in his own wisdom or his own powers of speech. Certainly Paul's talents were many, and they were enhanced and sanctified by God for sacred use. But he recognized the work he was involved in to be the work of the Holy Spirit.

The message of the cross needs no one to add his or her own wisdom to it. The message of the cross must not be altered to accommodate the thinking of the world just because we might think to make it less offensive or less strange to the ears of sinners.

The message of the cross is an offense by God's design. 1 Corinthians 1:18-25 says, "For the message of the cross is foolishness to those who are perishing, but to us who are being saved it is the power of God. For it is written: 'I will destroy the wisdom of the wise; the intelligence of the intelligent I will frustrate.' Where is the wise person? Where is the teacher of the law? Where is the philosopher of this age? Has not God made foolish the wisdom of the world? For since in the wisdom of God the world through its wisdom did not know him, God was pleased through the foolishness of what was preached to save those who believe. Jews demand signs and Greeks look for wisdom, but we preach Christ crucified: a stumbling block to Jews and foolishness to Gentiles, but to those whom God has called, both Jews and Greeks, Christ the power of God and the wisdom of God. For the foolishness of God is wiser than human wisdom, and the weakness of God is stronger than human strength."

Why is the message of the cross an offense, and necessarily so? Part of the answer can be found in 1 Corinthians 1:26-31, which says, "Brothers and sisters, think of what you were when you were called. Not many of you were wise by human standards; not many were influential; not many were of noble birth. But God chose the foolish things of the world to shame the wise; God chose the weak things of the world to shame the strong. God chose the lowly things of this world and the despised things—and the things that are not—to nullify the things that are, so that no one may boast before him. It is because of him that you are in Christ Jesus, who has become for us wisdom from God—that is, our righteousness, holiness and redemption. Therefore, as it is written: 'Let the one who boasts boast in the Lord.'"

Certainly the gospel is adaptable enough for presentation in any culture. But its truths and standards must not be changed to accommodate the fashions and feelings of the world. The message of the cross has been co-opted by many groups and causes, producing political theologies, social theologies, theistic evolution, humanistic religion, health and prosperity gospels, and cultural adaptations of Christianity. The gospel is modified by those who justify their versions with the claim that the gospel must be packaged for situational application in order for it to be effective. According to this way of thinking we must devise ways to make the gospel more effective, because on its own and in certain situations it is defective, inadequate, or in some way inappropriate.

Certainly we must always be concerned with relevance. But this is not achieved by compromising the message. Whenever the biblical message of the cross is made to conform to human wisdom, you have a distortion of the message. In 1 Corinthians 1:17 Paul asserted that he was called to preach the gospel—not with words of mere human wisdom, lest the cross of Christ be emptied of its power. If we add to or subtract from the gospel message, or present it in any way other than in its pure, straightforward, biblical form, we dilute it, change it into something else, and take away its power to save.

Other examples of this are certain brands of dispensationalism (those who make certain aspects of the Holy Spirit's activity outdated or defunct in this age), sexual liberation theology, statements of faith that downplay biblical inspiration and authority, the "God understands and won't send me to hell" attitude, the denials of miracles, and the unwillingness to talk about sin. We might be tempted to think that reaching new people requires avoidance of the topic of sin.

The message of the cross must always be declared as the Bible reveals it, not as we think it should be, and not as we think others would like to hear it. We should not find ourselves shrinking from or apologizing for its teachings. In doing so, we rob the message of its power. If we design a gospel that we think is a "reasonable" facsimile and more acceptable to ourselves and others, we neutralize the true gospel's divine power in our lives and in our witness. Trying to soften the message and ease its impact only destroys it. We end up with a religion without power to change lives. The gospel was designed by God, and we cannot improve upon it or alter it without lessening or even ruining its effectiveness. The true gospel is *always* powerful and effective. We can distinguish between our teaching and God's by the results. Sometimes the gospel message softens hearts, and at other times hearts are hardened. The message of the cross is not offensive because it is obnoxious, but because it is true! Let it remain so!

The heart of the message of the cross is to know Christ and the effect of His atoning work on our lives. No wisdom known to man can possibly be substituted. Eloquence, fame, comfort, and approval by man were not Paul's goal, but rather it was his aim to know Christ and Him crucified. Therefore he devoted himself to the message of the cross, which confounds all earthly wisdom, and in which is found the only power to make men and women wise unto salvation. Let us not preach some deficient, or even impotent, message. Many messages can gain followers, but only the true message of the cross can save souls!

If the true gospel of Jesus Christ will not convict, if it will not bring understanding, if it does not contain enough power and wisdom from God, if it is not effective to change hearts with God's love, then no other version of the message we try will work either. It is unnecessary to say, "In order to reach this audience I must fit the gospel to their expectations." The gospel is the power of God, and so it is able to break down any barrier just as it is. It is adaptable, but not changeable.

THE DEMONSTRATION OF THE MESSAGE

There are many voices that claim to declare the truth. I have often wondered how the unbeliever can ever hope to know which "gospel" is true. Christians of all different denominations, and religious groups like the Mormons, Jehovah's Witnesses,

Unification Church members, etc., pound on doors claiming to offer listeners the truth about God, man, spirituality, and the universe. How can anyone possibly know whom to believe? How do people know if the teachings of genuine Christian witnesses comprise the real truth, or merely another version? Why should anyone believe a Christian evangelist or preacher more than any other claimant to divine knowledge?

Let us not suppose that the sinful, unregenerate mind will be able to easily see the obvious superiority of the genuine Christian message. Every cult missionary knows his or her presentation well, including in it a mixture of concern, politeness, logic, and Bible texts. Christian witnesses appear to the public to be one group among many that claims to know the truth. Deep inside we know this, and many Christians hesitate to share their faith, lest they be viewed as only one in a long parade of "religious kooks."

If the evangelical Christian church really does have the truth, how can we convince the world of this? Is it a matter of method of presentation? Does it depend on a superior logic or eloquence on our part? Should we stay away from door to door evangelism or literature evangelism, or even sharing Christ with our friends? Is it something we ourselves must do that will reveal that we and our doctrine are different from others?

There is nothing we ourselves can do to achieve that sense of conviction in the heart of those to whom we preach and witness. But that does not mean we are in a hopeless situation. We are called upon to witness simply, boldly, straightforwardly, and lovingly. We should not resort to novel methods, gimmicks, or anything beyond the simple speaking forth of the gospel message of the cross of Jesus Christ.

Is it a matter of just witnessing with the rest of the pack of religious cults with the hope of getting our share of souls? No! For to those who share the truth of God's gospel, God has promised to add a supernatural ingredient that will do what we could never do ourselves, namely, convince our hearers that the word of truth we speak is different, that it is the genuine teaching of God for their lives. That is not to say that every instance of hearing the gospel will result in a conversion. But in this case the hearer's choice will not only be one of whether or not to believe a doctrinal presentation made by a man or woman, but of whether to accept or reject the working of God in their hearts through the spoken gospel.

Paul did not present the gospel with words of human wisdom and eloquence. There is nothing wrong with eloquence, but Paul realized that the success of his preaching did not ultimately depend on how well chosen his words were, how pleasing he made them sound, or how well he was able to conform them to the thinking of contemporary popular beliefs and ideas. The message of the cross must never be reduced to only that. Certainly the gospel was spoken in language readily understandable to Jewish and Greek cultures alike. It was adaptable, but never conformable. It still remained a stumbling block to worldly thinking, Jewish and Greek.

How did Paul present the message of the cross? In "weakness and trembling," that is, without dependence on his own power to make the message strong. Behind Paul's human frailty was God. Thus was he able to present the gospel "with a demonstration of the Spirit's power" (1 Corinthians 2:4).

The Spirit's power accompanies every witness to the true gospel. We have something no religion or cult has, namely, the working of the living Spirit of God. How do we convince the world our gospel is the truth? The answer: we don't. The Spirit convinces. How will our message stand out as different? The demonstration of the Spirit's power. We can go out with confidence, not intimidated by the skepticism of the world or the zeal of the cultists. We can go with confidence that the true gospel of Jesus Christ is powerful in itself, and that the Spirit of God works within it and us in a way no other religious group will ever experience or manifest.

The word "demonstration" means a pointing out, a showing. There are two ways the power of the Spirit of God is demonstrated in the course of a Christian sharing the gospel: 1) Conviction (this is the desired effect of the gospel on its hearers), and 2) Miracles. Let's look at each individually.

CONVICTION

In John 16:8-11 Jesus describes the role of the Holy Spirit in this way: "When he comes, he will prove the world to be in the wrong about sin and righteousness and judgment: about sin, because people do not believe in me; about righteousness, because I am going to the Father, where you can see me no longer; and about judgment, because the prince of this world now stands condemned."

This demonstration was in contrast with the methods of proof and philosophical arguments esteemed in Paul's day. The power did not lie in Paul's ability to persuade, but in the Spirit's ability to convict. According to Acts 1:8, it is this Spirit of conviction and power that makes us effective witnesses of Jesus Christ.

So, the faith of the believers was not a faith in Paul's wisdom or the wisdom of any other man, but it was faith in the power of God manifested in the telling of the message of the cross of Jesus Christ.

As a pastor I preach and teach and witness with the desire that the faith of my hearers will lie not in my seminary training or the logic of my presentation (though God can and does use such things). Rather, their faith must ultimately be in God and in the power of the cross of Christ, in the power demonstrated in the resurrection of Jesus, in the wisdom of God's Word, and in the conviction of the Holy Spirit.

In 1 Corinthians 10:10-12 we can see that Paul may not have measured up to the expectations of public oratory of his day. He did possess a certain eloquence and a great deal of depth, as we can see from his writings. But some of those who heard him speak did not seem to feel that he was equal to the golden-tongued speakers of that culture. As has been mentioned earlier in this book, for many what was said was not as important as how it was said. Not content and truth, but rather technique were exalted.

That did not matter to Paul. He did not attempt to imitate the oratory styles of the "stars" of his day. Paul only wanted to communicate the message of the cross and depend on the Holy Spirit to accomplish what only He could. He depended on the Holy Spirit to achieve the desired affect on his hearers. Paul did not go about this haphazardly, but he knew that only a divine message with a divine power could change lives. A human gospel, no matter how well thought out and delivered might produce followers and surface effects, but not salvation.

Man's logic can persuade other men to believe almost anything. But much more is at stake in the preaching of the gospel of salvation than producing mere agreement with our assertions. And more is at stake than mere approval of the listeners. Souls are at stake! And Paul believed that God placed supernatural power in His gospel, power to convict hearts. He believed that God stood behind the true gospel Himself in the person of His Spirit. But He does not stand behind another gospel (see Galatians 1:6-9).

To be an effective witness requires obedience (to live and speak the message of the cross) and trust (in God for the results), and not personal magnetism or even lengthy training. How this understanding should free anyone who wants to tell others about Jesus, but who hesitates because of perceived personal inadequacy, or who is intimidated by the hardened hearts of sinners! We are not the ones who accomplish the crucial work of conviction in the hearts of those to whom we speak! We only need surrender ourselves to be God's speakers and instruments! And we do not want anyone's faith to lie in our wisdom, but in God!

MIRACLES

Another way God causes the gospel to be demonstrated with power is through the accompaniment of attesting miracles. Mark 16:20 says, "Then the disciples went out and preached everywhere, and the Lord worked with them and confirmed his word by the signs that accompanied it."

In Acts 4:29-30 the disciples prayed, "Now, Lord, consider their threats and enable your servants to speak your word with great boldness. Stretch out your hand to heal and perform signs and wonders through the name of your holy servant Jesus." Verse 31 records the result: "After they prayed, the place where they were meeting was shaken. And they were all filled with the Holy Spirit and spoke the word of God boldly." Verse 33 says, "With great power the apostles continued to testify to the resurrection of the Lord Jesus. And God's grace was so powerfully at work in them all."

In Acts 14:3 we read, "So Paul and Barnabas spent considerable time there, speaking boldly for the Lord, who confirmed the message of his grace by enabling them to perform signs and wonders."

In Acts 2:22 Peter even says of Jesus, "Fellow Israelites, listen to this: Jesus of Nazareth was a man accredited by God to you by miracles, wonders and signs, which God did among you through him, as you yourselves know." In John 10:25 Jesus Himself said, "The works I do in my Father's name testify about me." (Compare

John 5:31-32,36-38; 8:14-18; 10:37-38; 20:30,31.)

We like to quote John 14:12, in which Jesus said, "Very truly I tell you, whoever believes in me will do the works I have been doing, and they will do even greater things than these, because I am going to the Father." Yet notice how frequently these works and miracles are connected with the sharing of the message of the cross. Indeed, the declaration of the message is the context for miracles, for they were most often given as God's confirmation that what a person was saying was true. The miracles of Jesus testified to the fact that He was who He said He was. The miracles of the early church were God's confirmations that their message was true. When Paul said that the preaching of his gospel was done in a demonstration of power, he was referring to conviction, to the power of God in changing lives, and also to miracles.

Often present-day Christians can be heard bemoaning the fact that the miracle-working power of God is not seen as much in today's church as it was in the days of the early church. Some have tried to explain it by saying that the age of miracles is over, that they accomplished their purpose in the first years of evangelization. Or they blame lack of faith. Or they accuse liberalism. And so forth.

First, Scripture nowhere suggests that the day would come when the demonstration of the genuineness of the gospel (as opposed to false gospels) by acts of divine power would come to an end. In this day of proliferation of false gospels and religions, a confirmation of the true message is needed more than ever. While lack of faith, sin in the church, liberal doctrines, etc., certainly do have their effect, let me suggest strongly what I believe to be a primary reason for the problem of powerlessness in the church today. It is simply this: we are not setting the context in which the Bible says miracles happen. That context includes a number of things (faith, holiness, compassion, to give some examples). But a major element of that context is the declaration of the Word of God to sinners, with the desired effect of seeing them come to a saving knowledge of and relationship with God through Jesus Christ.

Miracles were not given by God as ends in themselves. They were not done for wonder's sake alone. They were acts of compassion to be sure. But they were also signs of confirmation of the words preached and taught by believers, meant to give divine testimony to their message, so that listeners would believe the gospel. Miracles were done by God as a way of saying, "Of all the claims to truth in the world, this is the one you can believe." Someone would preach, teach, or witness to the gospel, and God would add His "amen" to the believer's words with a demonstration of power.

Though there are exceptions, much of what Christians do occurs within the "walls" of the church. Christians speak much to each other. Our books and music are mostly sold in Christian bookstores to other Christians. We preach on Christian television stations watched primarily by Christians. We testify to each other in our worship services. But how much are we taking the message to the sinner where he or she is? What "word" of witness does God have to confirm?

The book of Acts records the earliest days of the church. That church was *characterized* by a great zeal to share the gospel with others. Their witness was accompanied (confirmed) by divine power. Their evangelism was natural, not imposed or urged on. As time went on, the church became enmeshed in organizational priorities. Human hierarchies were set up in place of the Headship of Jesus Christ. Human machinery took the place of the administration of the Word and Spirit of God. The church became preoccupied with the survival of the systems of "churchianity" it had invented for itself. *It was no longer a church on mission*. Indeed, it can be seriously doubted whether much of what passed for the church was Christ's church at all. (NOTE: I am speaking generally; I do not believe in the "complete apostasy of the church." This would make Jesus' prediction in Matthew 16:18 a failure.) Much of the church's energies were absorbed into the maintenance of the organization. No longer was its primary focus the declaration of the gospel to any who would hear. And without that vital witness, the context for miracles was absent.

Many of the important reformations that have taken place since the sixteenth century have produced a "mission-oriented" zeal. They were originally evangelistic and missionary in purpose. Along with this reformation mind-set, it was not uncommon to observe a renewal of spiritual power. This author stands with the Church of God Reformation Movement, which began late in the nineteenth century. As with other movements, its beginnings were marked with very little emphasis on organization, but with great urgency on sharing their message of salvation, holiness, and the oneness of the church. And accompanying the activities of what they termed "the flying ministry" were many testimonies of physical healing and other miracles. Since its early days the Church of God Reformation Movement has become more settled in terms of organization, and predictably, the frequency of miracles has decreased. I am encouraged whenever I see efforts being made to revive our evangelistic focus. I believe that as our movement, or any truly Christian movement of God's Spirit, or any congregation, takes on or recaptures the evangelistic spirit, God will confirm our testimony with demonstrations of the power of His Spirit.

I observe that the church's voice is being heard with greater effect regarding certain moral issues. There are outcries against pornography, abortion, humanistic indoctrination in the public schools, state and federal infringement on religious and family rights, gratuitous sex and violence in the entertainment media, occultism in children's entertainment, and so on. I am glad this is happening. Let the reader understand that I am for the Christian being involved in fighting for moral legislation, writing letters to Congressmen, and refusing to do business with companies that sponsor immorality and violence. We must make our voice heard on such matters. Perhaps these are the best ways for visibly accomplishing some immediate results in specific areas of concern.

But I am concerned at the same time that many Christians may believe that these sorts of efforts will make the ultimate difference. In the end, while it is possible to enact moral legislation, it is impossible to legislate practical morality. Laws are passed every day and promptly disobeyed. Sinful man rebels against law, God's law and civil law. If you cut off one route of sin and crime, it will find another way. Create a vacuum, and something will fill it.

The ultimate answer to the sin problem is to change lives. While I am not advocating that Christians forsake their involvement in getting moral laws passed and enforced, neither do I want Christians to place their ultimate hopes in these things, for there is something more powerful. It is something ordained by God to bring permanent results in our efforts to change the world—by changing one heart at a time. What is that method? Tell people the gospel of Jesus Christ, boldly and lovingly and urgently! I will even go so far as to say that believers must not expend their *best* time, energy, and resources on anything other than telling anyone who will listen about Jesus Christ. Not all will be saved, but more will be saved by speaking than by not speaking. The early church went forth conquering for Jesus, not by being social activists, but by declaring the good news of salvation.

For this task, we must have absolute faith in the power of the gospel to save. We must view the message of the cross as the most powerful means God has put at our disposal to change people and nations.

When the church of Jesus Christ learns that the lifestyle of the cross means natural, lifestyle evangelism (sharing Christ by our life and our verbal witness every day, because that is who and what we are), then the Spirit will confirm our holy lives and our words of testimony with a work of conviction in human hearts and with manifestations of His reality through miracles, the combined effect of which will result in new believers. The lifestyle of the cross necessarily includes the bearing of the message about Jesus Christ. You cannot leave the sharing of the message out of your daily Christian walk, nor can you dilute the message to suit your hearers.

2 Corinthians 4:13-14 says, "It is written: 'I believed; therefore I have spoken.' Since we have that same spirit of faith, we also believe and therefore speak, because we know that the one who raised the Lord Jesus from the dead will also raise us with Jesus and present us with you to himself."

LET THE CHURCH SPEAK WHAT IT BELIEVES!

Chapter Five

The Wisdom of God

Do you remember the message you received when you first believed? Included in that message was some word about the cross of Christ. Included in that message was the good news of God's love in Christ as demonstrated in the cross.

In seminary I studied homiletics under Dr. James Massey. He stressed his conviction that a sermon that does not mention the cross of Christ is not truly a Christian sermon. That idea has always stayed with me. If the message of the cross is not heard through a sermon or teaching, then that sermon or teaching is not truly Christian.

Think of your lost loved ones, friends, neighbors, fellow-workers, and the strangers you come into contact with every day. Do you have a burden for their souls? If not, you will feel no urgency to share the gospel of Christ with them. If you do carry a burden for souls, let me emphasize to you that no person will get saved without hearing the gospel. And that gospel must not be yours or mine. It must be the gospel of Jesus Christ as revealed in the Bible.

Do you believe that, just as the message of the cross was a powerful instrument to lead you to accept Christ as your Savior, it is also able to lead others to Christ? There is power and wisdom in the message of the cross, because the content of that message is Jesus Christ, who is the power and wisdom of God (1 Corinthians 1:30). The wisdom of the gospel is different from our wisdom. It is different from the world's wisdom. It is wisdom given from above to accomplish the purpose of redemption, a work of God beyond our ability to understand or plan.

If you are a Christian, you are so because of the effect of this divine wisdom contained in the message of the cross. And now you are called upon to be a bearer of the word about the cross. Think again of those lost loved ones and neighbors. God has made His people the bearers of the message of salvation on earth. Yes, cross-bearing includes bearing the *message* of the cross.

Let's look at the biblical description of the wisdom of the message of the cross. Look again at 1 Corinthians 1:18-30 (quoted in the last chapter). God has made the wisdom of this world nothing. How? By sending His Son to be crucified. That divine act of love defies all worldly wisdom. It brings to nothing all religious merit. It contradicted even the religious expectations of Jesus' day. The sight of Jesus nailed to the cross proved to the Jews and Romans that He could not be what He claimed, for this could never happen to the Messiah. The Jews expected a military leader, a conqueror of the Gentiles. They did not expect a Messiah sent to free people from their most deadly enemy—sin.

But this was God's wisdom. We never would have thought of it or expected it. It is beyond human reason or comprehension.

What is wisdom? Is it synonymous with human reasoning, planning, or perceptions? Heavenly wisdom may actually contradict these things. Indeed, divine wisdom and earthly wisdom are contrasted in the Scriptures as two entirely different things (James 3:13-18). God's wisdom will always be different than the wisdom of unregenerate minds. 1 Corinthians 2:6-16; 3:18-20 says, "We do, however, speak a message of wisdom among the mature, but not the wisdom of this age or of the rulers of this age, who are coming to nothing. No, we declare God's wisdom, a mystery that has been hidden and that God destined for our glory before time began. None of the rulers of this age understood it, for if they had, they would not have crucified the Lord of glory. However, as it is written: 'What no eye has seen, what no ear has heard, and what no human mind has conceived'—the things God has prepared for those who love him—these are the things God has revealed to us by his Spirit. The Spirit searches all things, even the deep things of God. For who knows a person's thoughts except their own spirit within them? In the same way no one knows the thoughts of God except the Spirit of God. What we have received is not the spirit of the world, but the Spirit who is from God, so that we may understand what God has freely given us. This is what we speak, not in words taught us by human wisdom but in words taught by the Spirit, explaining spiritual realities with Spirit-taught words. The person without the Spirit does not accept the things that come from the Spirit of God but considers them foolishness, and cannot understand them because they are discerned only through the Spirit. The person with the Spirit makes judgments about all things, but such a person is not subject to merely human judgments, for, 'Who has known the mind of the Lord so as to instruct him?' But we have the mind of Christ. . . .

"Do not deceive yourselves. If any of you think you are wise by the standards of this age, you should become 'fools' so that you may become wise. For the wisdom of this world is foolishness in God's sight. As it is written: 'He catches the wise in their craftiness'; and again, 'The Lord knows that the thoughts of the wise are futile.'"

This has two important implications:

1. Sinful man cannot, by his own power, understand the wisdom of the gospel.

2. We cannot change the gospel to accommodate the world's wisdom, or it will no longer be the wisdom of God we are presenting.

This does not mean that sinful men cannot come to know the truth of the gospel. But in order for them to do that, the Holy Spirit must be there to convict them, to draw them. In John 6:44, Jesus said, "No one can come to me unless the Father who sent me draws them." The Father draws people by His Spirit. If they respond to this opening of their spiritual eyes they may be saved.

Where has human wisdom brought us? Worldly wisdom presents us with a distorted sense of justice and ethics. It warps our beliefs about what is right and wrong. It leads men and women to justify abortion by calling it "pro-choice." It helps society defend homosexuality as another normal sexual alternative. On the one hand the homosexual community does not want to be victimized by societal mores; and on the other hand, they defend themselves by asserting that they are mere victims of random genetic heredity. This removes sin from the category of morals and ethics, and defends it by representing it as mere animal instinct, while in the same breath claiming to stand for human dignity.

Worldly wisdom calls degrading pornography "art." Human wisdom has warned us against disciplining our children, lest we thwart their "creativity" (the new term for "misbehavior"). Human wisdom brings us to the belief that the universe came together by a long series of accidents. It calls for a ban on children praying over their lunches at school. It promotes violence as a form of entertainment, even for our young.

The wisdom of the world can never lead anyone to God. For one thing, we could never have imagined God's plan of salvation as revealed in the suffering of Christ on the cross. Our wisdom and knowledge can never discover God in such a way as to lead to a personal relationship with Him. One might look at the order of the universe and know there must be a God (Romans 1:19-20), but in order to know what God is like and what His will is for us, God had to reveal Himself and His will to us in a special way. He has done this through His revealed Word, the Bible; and He has revealed Himself supremely and finally in His Son Jesus Christ. Jesus Christ embodies the message of the cross, preserved for us in Scripture.

Human wisdom is ineffective to represent spiritual things (things of the Spirit of God). Our wisdom tends toward supporting our own desires and plans and justifying our own sins (sometimes under the guise of religion). But God in His mercy sent His Word, His self-revelation, and that Word became flesh and dwelt among us as the Son of God. By God's will Jesus died on the cross for our sins, was raised to life on the third day, ascended to the right hand of the Father in heaven, and now, through His Spirit, persistently calls us to Himself. All this is God's wisdom. Jesus is God's wisdom. And Jesus has become our wisdom, if we accept Him as Savior and Lord. Otherwise, we are left with own futile groping after something true.

For the Jews, the cross of Christ was a stumbling block, an offense, a scandal. The Greek word for "stumbling block" in 1 Corinthians 1:23 is *skandalon*, from which our English word "scandal" is derived. Their law said that anyone who was hanged on a tree was cursed (Deuteronomy 21:23; compare Galatians 3:13). They did not understand that it was *their* curse (and ours) that Jesus took upon Himself, and not His own. He was without sin. Indeed, this fact qualified Him to die for our sins, since He had no sins of His own to atone for. The messiah the Jews were expecting would show himself mighty in worldly concerns (military victory and political reign). How could He say something like, "My kingdom is not of this world" (John 18:36)?

To the Greeks, the gospel message was not wise, or philosophical enough. The love for complicated systems of belief can often cause people to reject the simplicity of salvation by the free grace of God. Not only must there be more to it than that, they reason, but an elaborate system of hypothesis and speculation provides more enjoyment to the human ego.

The Greeks could not see the sense in a gospel that portrayed God as loving the world so much that He would send His only begotten Son to die. They preferred to think of God as a transcendent being or force who was unaffected by human suffering. God went about His own business.

Today many still have trouble believing that God, who does not suffer physically or mentally, would be understanding enough of our human dilemma to be as radically involved in our situation as the gospel teaches that He is. It is easier to view God as a "force," or as someone who is generally absent from the creation He made. This also helps free the sinner from the moral obligations the gospel puts him under. (See Psalm 10:1-6,11,13-14; Isaiah 29:15-16; Zephaniah 1:12.)

The Greek gnostic sects believed that the flesh was inherently and incurably evil, and therefore God would never come in the flesh. They denied that Jesus was the Lord. John spoke to this error in 1 John 4:1-3 went he wrote: "Dear friends, do not believe every spirit, but test the spirits to see whether they are from God, because many false prophets have gone out into the world. This is how you can recognize the Spirit of God: Every spirit that acknowledges that Jesus Christ has come in the flesh is from God, but every spirit that does not acknowledge Jesus is not from God. This is the spirit of the antichrist, which you have heard is coming and even now is already in the world."

To the Greek's preference of eloquent oratorical expression over content the blunt proclamation of Christianity would have seemed nonsensical and ridiculously simple.

Think again of lost souls you know. They have some system of thought and belief, some philosophy, some theology, that helps them to justify their lives. But the Holy Spirit can break through all of that and speak to their hearts. He has chosen to do that through the message of the cross and the other-worldly wisdom of the gospel. He does not use a message that conforms to the ways people want to think (though the gospel is adaptable to cultures, it is not conformable in terms of its message), but rather He uses the simple message of Christ's love and sacrifice for sin. Don't be embarrassed by the simple wisdom of the message of the cross, but speak it boldly and lovingly and urgently, for God has made His true followers the bearers of the message.

Consider the example of Paul as you accomplish your role as a bearer of God's wisdom. In 1 Corinthians 2:2 he wrote: "For I resolved to know nothing while I was with you except Jesus Christ and him crucified." And again in 1 Corinthians 4:1-6 he wrote: "This, then, is how you ought to regard us: as servants of Christ and as those entrusted with the mysteries God has revealed. Now it is required that those who have been given a trust must prove faithful. I care very little if I am judged by you or by any human court; indeed, I do not even judge myself. My conscience is clear, but that does not make me innocent. It is the Lord who judges me. Therefore judge nothing before the appointed time; wait until the Lord comes. He will bring to light what is hidden in darkness and will expose the motives of the heart. At that time each will receive their praise from God. Now, brothers and sisters, I have applied these things to myself and Apollos for your benefit, so that you may learn from us the meaning of the saying, 'Do not go beyond what is written.'"

Paul wrote that those things of God deemed foolish or weak by men are still wiser and stronger than anything that is thought up by man. In the message of the cross resides the power and wisdom of God, a wisdom that is active, for its content is Jesus Christ, who lives and is the power and wisdom of God. You cannot improve upon it. You can trust it. You can be confident in sharing it.

The message of the cross led to our salvation when we were saved. If we want to see others saved (and that should be our highest priority in the world), we must give them the word about the cross and resurrection of Jesus Christ. If you are saved, you have been entrusted with God's Word and message and wisdom and power for other souls. Paul wrote to Timothy about the treasure of the gospel he had received. 1 Timothy 6:20 says, "Timothy, guard what has been entrusted to your care." And he wrote in 2 Timothy 1:13-14, "What you heard from me, keep as the pattern of sound teaching, with faith and love in Christ Jesus. Guard the good deposit that was entrusted to you—guard it with the help of the Holy Spirit who lives in us." To "guard" the gospel means to keep it pure and unchanged. It does not mean to keep it to ourselves. Rather, Romans 10:13-15 instructs us to share it with those who need to know Jesus as Savior: "'Everyone who calls on the name of the Lord will be saved.' How, then, can they call on the one they have not believed in? And how can they believe in the one of whom they have not heard? And how can they hear without someone preaching to them? And how can anyone preach unless they are sent? As it is written: 'How beautiful are the feet of those who bring good news!'" Note that the word "preach" in this passage does not refer only to formal sermons or pulpit preaching. The word means to "declare," an activity not reserved only for the pulpit, but something to be engaged in by all believers in winning souls for Christ.

To live the lifestyle of the cross (which is the only life of discipleship Jesus accepts as genuine) we must be bearers of the wisdom of God, which is the message of the cross. Because the message is contrary to worldly wisdom, you may meet with negative attitudes, but if you trust in the power of God residing in the gospel, you can bear the Word of God to others confidently.

Chapter Six

Portraits of Christ

The way Christ is portrayed is of utmost importance. Paul, frustrated because of the confusion certain men were causing in the Galatian church, said, "You foolish Galatians! Who has bewitched you? Before your very eyes Jesus Christ was clearly portrayed as crucified" (Galatians 3:1). This portrayal of Christ having been crucified is the heart of the Christian message, and therefore the foundation of the Christian way of life. But, human wisdom can dilute or change the message, emptying it of its power. The message, which describes the atoning work of Christ on the cross, must be presented faithfully in word and living. Our portrayal of Christ is crucial to the purity and effectiveness of the message. If one's Christology is faulty, so is the rest of one's understanding of biblical doctrine.

The message of the cross is sometimes diluted in certain Christian sects, but the greatest distortion is found in the teachings of the so-called cults. Many of these groups declare that they are Christian and freely use the name of Christ. Many claim to revere the Bible. But the most important question to ask of any belief system, especially one calling itself Christian, is: are they preaching the biblical Christ who is portrayed in Scripture as the

One who was crucified for our sins? Does the group give the cross of Christ the meaning the biblical gospel gives to it? Or is the Christ they preach a different Christ?

In 2 Corinthians 11:4 Paul takes to task those who are preaching a different Jesus than the one witnessed to by the apostles. "For is someone comes to you and preaches a Jesus other than the Jesus we preached, or if you receive a different spirit from the Spirit you received, or a different gospel from the one you accepted, you put up with it easily enough."

There are many counterfeit gospels that present counterfeit christs, a different Spirit, and what passes for the church. Compare this was Galatians 1:6-9, where Paul wrote, "I am astonished that you are so quickly deserting the one who called you to live in the grace of Christ and are turning to a different gospel—which is really no gospel at all. Evidently some people are throwing you into confusion and are trying to pervert the gospel of Christ. But even if we or an angel from heaven should preach a gospel other than the one we preached to you, let them be under God's curse! As we have already said, so now I say again: If anybody is preaching to you a gospel other than what you accepted, let them be under God's curse!"

How can we tell the difference between one claim to the truth and another? Every "gospel" must be compared with what the Bible actually says. Compare each statement with the whole Word of God, remembering that many of the cults quote copiously from the Bible, taking passages out of context in much the same way Satan did when tempting Jesus in the desert (Matthew 4). It is necessary to have a good knowledge of the whole Bible.

Read the Bible prayerfully, relying on the Holy Spirit to teach you its truths (1 John 2:20). An unregenerate mind cannot judge Scripture correctly, nor can it guarantee the ability to discern between competing claims to truth. A member of the Unification

Church rejected my attempts to show him texts from the Bible. He said that he believed God spoke not only through the Bible but through other "scriptures" as well. When I asked him what standard he used to test claims to truth, he replied that he knew something was true when it "felt right" in his heart. I pointed out to him that without an objective measuring stick for truth, he was apt to believe anything that felt right at the time. (Reread chapter four of this book.)

One of the most important things to consider about any group's teaching is their portrayal of Christ. Again, if one's view of Christ is not correct, the rest of one's belief system is wrong. Many groups claim to be representing Jesus, yet they offer many contradictory versions of Christ. Understanding correctly the way the Bible presents Christ is fundamental to testing the truth of a doctrinal system. I urge the reader to read this chapter with an open Bible at hand. Remember that the lifestyle of the cross (the authentic Christian walk) is the only kind of discipleship Jesus accepts, and this kind of discipleship is based on the true message of the cross, which portrays Christ as crucified. What follows is important because without the correct portrayal of Christ, discipleship is based on wrong information.

THE CHURCH OF JESUS CHRIST OF LATTER DAY SAINTS (MORMONS)

The LDS church claims that the Bible is one of their scriptural sources, but they add other so-called "revelations," namely *The Book of Mormon, Doctrine and Covenants*, and *Pearl of Great Price*. These were allegedly written by Joseph Smith, who claimed to be a prophet sent by God to restore the gospel to its fullness. The latter two writings in particular contradict many teachings of the Bible, even though the Mormons claim that all four books are inspired scripture. How do they reconcile this fact?

Mormon Article of Faith number eight states: "We believe the Bible to be the true word of God as far as it is translated correctly." If the Bible disagrees with Smith's teachings, they simply assert that the Bible *would* agree if it were accurately translated at that point. Even though the Mormons declare their reverence for the Bible as the Word of God and list it among their scriptures, they actually do not trust the Bible. They declare that dishonest men down through the ages deliberately changed and deleted passages, leaving us with a distorted version. This is why God sent Joseph Smith to "restore" the gospel and the church. This effectively robs the Bible of its power, because if there is doubt about one part of it, the whole is brought into question. So, while claiming to revere the Bible, they actually destroy its credibility.

As one who believes that the Bible is the inspired Word of God, I firmly believe that the Spirit who saw to it that God's Word was given to man is fully capable of preserving it down through history. The discovery of thousands of copies and partial copies in manuscript form testify to the amazing accuracy of the transmission of Scripture from ancient times. On the other hand, *The Book of Mormon* has no such corroboration, either in ancient manuscripts or archeological discoveries.

What do Mormonism and its writings teach about Jesus? They claim to believe in the same Savior Christians put their faith in, but is the Mormon Jesus the same Jesus the Bible reveals, or one of the "different" christs mentioned in 2 Corinthians 11:3?

Mormonism teaches that Jesus is divine. But rather than revealing the one true God in the flesh, he is one god among many gods. He is the spirit child of Elohim. Lucifer is his spirit brother. He is not the same as the Father, but another god altogether. Not only is this a denial of the Trinity and a promotion of polytheism, but is also means that the God who created us (identified in the

Old Testament as Elohim) did not come Himself to accomplish our atonement through suffering, but He sent a substitute. Rather than die Himself, He sent another god. In the Christian faith, we believe that the Father and the Son are two Persons in the one Godhead. They are one God, not two.

The LDS church teaches that Jesus was the son of Elohim, who was an exalted man still possessing a body of flesh and bones, and had intercourse with the virgin Mary, who was promised to Joseph. He did this because He wanted to provide a body for His spirit son, Jesus.

The Bible teaches that through the miraculous power of the Holy Spirit (the third Person of the Trinity), the human life of Jesus was created within the womb of Mary without any sexual activity taking place with any man (human or exalted). There is no way at all that any of the gospel writings could be construed any other way. Jesus declared in John 4 that God is Spirit. The Bible also declares that God is not a man (Numbers 23:19). The Mormons, in making God an exalted man, are not presenting any biblical portrayal of the Lord.

The Mormon Savior is not the second Person of the Godhead. He is the first-born spirit child of Elohim and one of his goddess wives. He is the devil's older brother. Some Mormons even go so far as to suggest that Jesus married both of the Marys and Martha, mentioned in the gospels as His followers, thus representing Him as a polygamist.

Brigham Young, the second prophet of the LDS church, stated that the sacrifice Jesus made on the cross by the shedding of His blood was ineffective for the cleansing of some sin. There are sins for which men must atone for by the shedding of their own blood. The Bible says, "But if we walk in the light, as he is in the light, we have fellowship with one another, and the blood of Jesus, his Son, purifies us from all sin" (1 John 1:7).

The Mormon teaching about Jesus would rob the cross of its full power because it contains a doctrine of partial salvation by the blood of Jesus.

JEHOVAH'S WITNESSES

Jehovah's Witnesses teach that Jesus is divine, but that He is a lesser god, created by Jehovah originally as the archangel Michael. In becoming a man He was known as Jesus, the Son of God. He attained godhood by volunteering to be our Savior. God Himself did not come as our Savior; He sent a lesser being.

The Watchtower Society teaches that Jesus was the Son of God, but not God Himself. He was originally a spirit person but was turned into flesh. The man Jesus died, but the flesh was not resurrected to life. Rather, Jesus rose a spirit-creature.

The Jehovah's Witness organization does not teach the eternality of Christ's Sonship, the complete divinity of Christ during the Incarnation, or the actual physical victory of Jesus over death through a literal bodily resurrection. Jesus was a master of disguise. He took on the appearance of a man and appeared to rise from the dead.

The Jehovah's Witnesses are a polytheistic cult. For them atonement is said to be incomplete until the Millennium. There is no perfect salvation at present. Again, the cross is robbed of its power.

CHRISTIAN SCIENCE

Christian Science denies the Trinity and the full deity of Christ. They teach that God is Mind. Jesus was a man who demonstrated Christ, but was not identical to the Christ. In fact, the Christ is actually a principle, an impersonal force, or a state of believing. Christian Science adherents teach that Jesus was a fallible man and not God. He was merely a human prophet who had discovered more than anyone else in history the Christ Principle. In other words, He was the greatest "Christian Scientist" who ever lived. He healed people of their illnesses by simply refusing to believe in sickness. He raised people from the dead by simply refusing to believe in death.

According to church of Christian Science there is no such thing as sin. Those who believe in sin are in error. Since all is from Mind (God), there can be no such thing as sin. The blood of Christ does not cleanse from sin. Jesus did not die for our sins. In fact, Jesus appeared to suffer only to show how terrible error of perception is; but He didn't really suffer, for there is no such thing as suffering. Jesus only appeared to suffer on the cross. He never died, since there is no such thing as death. He was alive all the time in the tomb, because death is not real. And finally, Jesus' resurrection was only staged to show the unreality of human material sense.

The cross is made superfluous in Christian Science. It was a deception to prove a point. There is no salvation, because salvation is not needed. And again, the cross is robbed of its power.

SPIRITISM

One of the principles of spiritism is that of personal responsibility. We alone are responsible for getting rid of our sins. The blood of Christ is not effective for that. There is no vicarious death for the sins of man.

I visited a spiritist campground in Indiana once, and there is a large statue of Jesus on the grounds. People carry Bibles and wear crosses. But Jesus is not the Son of God. He was only a great teacher and spiritist (after all, He spoke to Moses and Elijah). Spiritists deny Jesus' deity and make Him to be a man only. A spiritist hymnbook contains the well-known hymn "Just As I Am," but the words are changed to read as follows:

Just as I am, without one plea,
But that, O God, Thou madest me.
And that my life is found in Thee
O God of love, I come, I come.

Reference to the shed blood of Christ is removed. He is not viewed as the Lamb of God who takes away the sins of the world. There is no message of the cross.

ARMSTRONGISM

This group calls itself the Worldwide Church of God, and was founded by the late Herbert W. Armstrong. It teaches the future divinity of all believers. Christ *became* a son of God only after the resurrection from the dead, and so will we. Jesus alone has been saved so far, being resurrected. However, He was not resurrected in the same body in which He died.

There is the usual denial of the Godhead. In fact, Armstrongism teaches that God cannot be limited to three persons.

For the Worldwide Church of God salvation involves works of the law. They teach that it is ridiculous to suppose that salvation is free. They have contempt for the doctrine of salvation by grace through faith. Rather, each us must work hard and hope we will be saved. No one will know whether or not they are saved until the resurrection. Indeed, no one is saved until the resurrection takes place.

This group claims that the teaching that Christ completed the plan of salvation on the cross is false. You cannot just believe and be saved. Nor does the blood of Christ finally save anyone. Christ only atones for past sins.

Here is what the Bible teaches: "But he [Christ] has appeared once for all at the culmination of the ages to do away with sin by the sacrifice of himself" (Hebrews 9:26).

(Note: the WCG is now also known as Grace Communion International, or GCI.)

THE UNIFICATION CHURCH

Sun Myung Moon claimed to have had a vision at the age of sixteen in which Christ appeared to him and told him that He had died before actually completing His entire mission. He had chosen Moon to complete that mission. Thus, Moon is believed by his followers to be the Christ of the Second Advent. Jesus Christ is not literally coming back to earth. When Jesus predicted His return, He was referring to His choosing of a successor to finish His mission. That person is identified as Sun Moon.

The cross is again robbed of its power. If Moon is to be believed, Christ did not accomplish our whole salvation on the cross, but only a part of it; Jesus did win a spiritual salvation for us, but He was supposed to marry and have children, thus beginning a new race of sinless people having no need of salvation. But He died prematurely, something outside His control, and did not win physical redemption for us.

This is but a sampling of how the cross is robbed of its power to save through false teachings about who Jesus Christ is and what He did.

I have given some extreme examples, but we could easily turn to some Christian theologies taught in denominational churches today that in more subtle ways undermine the full power of the cross. All of the above examples portray a different Christ. We can also weaken the power of the cross by softening what the true Jesus accomplished through His death.

After declaring cursed anyone who preaches a different gospel than the one he had preach to them, Paul wrote in Galatians 1:10-12, "Am I now trying to win the approval of human beings, or of God? Or am I trying to please people? If

I were still trying to please people, I would not be a servant of Christ."

The true word of the cross, as found in the pages of the Bible, is our standard for discerning truth from falsehood. This word must be accompanied by listening to the Holy Spirit as we prayerfully study the Bible. Each of the above religious groups claims to use the Bible, but they only use the portions that appear to support their claims. We must be concerned with being familiar with the whole council of God given in His Word. It is too easy for human wisdom and desires to adulterate the real message of the Bible, thus emptying it of its power.

1 John 4:1,4-6 says, "Dear friends, do not believe every spirit, but test the spirits to see whether they are from God, because many false prophets have gone out into the world. . . . You, dear children, are from God and have overcome them, because the one who is in you is greater than the one who is in the world. They are from the world and therefore speak from the viewpoint of the world, and the world listens to them. We are from God, and whoever knows God listens to us; but whoever is not from God does not listen to us. This is how we recognize the Spirit of truth and the spirit of falsehood."

There is a strong spirit of error in the world today. The church of God must resort to the Spirit of truth speaking through the revealed Word of God. Jesus said the Spirit would be our Teacher. This involves both knowing the truth and being empowered to live the truth in a way that God is demonstrating His power in these earthen vessels (2 Corinthians 4:7).

Let us devote ourselves more fully and carefully to knowing and practicing the truth, to study and to prayer, and to spreading the true message of the cross everywhere. This is the urgent business of every true believer. False teachings are abounding more and more. How much greater is our message! It has the power to save those who believe.

In Romans 1:16 Paul declared, "For I am not ashamed of the gospel, because it is the power of God that brings salvation to everyone who believes." Let us be determined in imitation of the apostle to know nothing among the people of this world, be they religious or irreligious, but Jesus Christ and Him crucified. In the face of so many portraits of Christ, let us portray the crucified One faithfully. This is the lifestyle of the cross!

Chapter Seven

Crucified with Christ

*L*iving the lifestyle of the cross is letting Christ live His life through us. This takes a genuine surrender to His will, devotion to His purposes, and belief in His atoning work on the cross for all people. Followers of Jesus believe that the crucifixion of Jesus was effective for our salvation. But that effectiveness lies in the fact that through the cross Jesus dealt directly with our sinful nature, which had dominion over us. As we believed in Christ's work on the cross, identifying His death as being the death we deserved and He suffered on our behalf, and as we believed and identified in His resurrection from the dead to conquer our final enemy (death), through faith we in fact participated in His death and resurrection. This means we allowed these events to touch us directly and change our lives.

To let Jesus Christ live through us involves a vital union with Him, a union by faith with Him in His death, resurrection, and present life.

In Romans 6:3-14 Paul wrote, "Or don't you know that all of us who were baptized into Christ Jesus were baptized into his death? We were therefore buried with him through baptism into death in order that, just as Christ was raised from the dead through the glory of the Father, we too may live a new life.

"For if we have been united with him in a death like his, we will certainly also be united with him in a resurrection like his. For we know that our old self was crucified with him so that the body ruled by sin might be done away with, that we should no longer be slaves to sin—because anyone who has died has been set free from sin.

"Now if we died with Christ, we believe that we will also live with him. For we know that since Christ was raised from the dead, he cannot die again; death no longer has mastery over him. The death he died, he died to sin once for all; but the life he lives, he lives to God.

"In the same way, count yourselves dead to sin but alive to God in Christ Jesus. Therefore do not let sin reign in your mortal body so that you obey its evil desires. Do not offer any part of yourself to sin as an instrument of wickedness, but rather offer yourselves to God as those who have been brought from death to life; and offer every part of yourself to him as an instrument of righteousness. For sin shall no longer be your master, because you are not under law, but under grace."

Paul used the familiar act of baptism to illustrate the reality of our union with Jesus in His death and life. Perhaps you have read or heard the familiar phrase, "Baptism is the outward sign of an inward grace." In other words, baptism is meant to depict by an outward act something real that has happened on the inside, in the soul. That depiction is of a cleansing from sin. In baptism we obey Christ's command to witness to our faith in His cleansing work in our hearts. We witness to our acceptance of all Christ has done for us. But Paul here gives us some further truth regarding the meaning of baptism.

In New Testament Greek the word translated "baptize" means to dip or immerse. First, Paul mentions the fact that we have been baptized into Christ. We have been joined with Jesus through our faith and through our obedience to undergo baptism. Though the actual act of baptism is certainly alluded to here, Paul's point is that Christians have been immersed in Christ. We have been joined with Christ inside and out.

Paul set forth the symbolism of something that has genuinely happened to those who have taken Christ as their Savior. Immersion under the water is a type or picture of a burial. We have put to death and are burying our former life without Christ. Coming up again out of the water is a picture of a resurrection. We have been raised to a new life in Christ. The life that is raised is not the life that was buried. It is a brand new life that comes forth. It is a different life. The old life remains dead and buried. Thus, when we become Christians, we have already experienced a death and a resurrection. We have left the old life behind. Our life started over completely. It is not only a new life, it is a new kind of life. It is eternal life, life from God, life that is lasting and of Christ-like quality and purpose.

2 Corinthians 5:17 says, "Therefore, if anyone is in Christ, the new creation has come: The old has gone, the new is here!" In Romans 6:6 Paul put it this way: "For we know that our old self was crucified with him so that the body ruled by sin might be done away with, that we should no longer be slaves to sin." In Galatians 2:20 Paul declared, "I have been crucified with Christ and I no longer live, but Christ lives in me. The life I now live in the body, I live by faith in the Son of God, who loved me and gave himself for me." He further said in Galatians 5:24, "Those who belong to Christ Jesus have crucified the flesh with its passions and desires." In the next chapter he wrote, "May I never boast except in the cross of our Lord Jesus Christ, through

which the world has been crucified to me, and I to the world" (6:14).

In determining to know nothing before the world but Christ and Him crucified, Paul was determined to both speak and display through his life the message of the cross. He declared in Colossians 2:20, "You died with Christ to the elemental spiritual forces of this world." And in Colossians 3:3,5 he again told the church, "For you died, and your life is now hidden with Christ in God. . . . Put to death, therefore, whatever belongs to your earthly nature."

We have union with Christ in this life when we so identify ourselves with His cross that His crucifixion becomes part of us, its effects being appropriated to us by faith. Then the Spirit of God applies the power of the cross to our lives. It was for our sins He died, and for Him we now live.

The union we have with Christ begins with the union we have with Him in His crucifixion. We escaped the tortures of the physical cross, but we do not escape crucifixion. Our old self must die in order for us to be in Christ. In justifying us God not only forgave us but also broke the dominion of sin over our lives. He further sanctifies us to remove the sinful nature, the bent toward sin, which answers to the temptations and offerings of this world system. By faith we entered intimately into Christ's death. So, Paul says, we must consider ourselves dead to sin, that sin might not rule us again. We must put our faith in Christ to do a perfect work in our hearts and not leave us in any respect in a state of servitude to sin.

This is contradictory to the commonly heard teaching that sin is inevitable in this life. Although sin is not impossible for a Christian, neither is it inevitable. 2 Corinthians 5:17 should be taken literally when it says, "Therefore, if anyone is in Christ, the new creation has come: The old has *gone*, the new is here!"

The sinful nature takes advantage of the weakness of the flesh, manifesting itself in the submission of the self to sinful desires. It is indwelling sin that shows itself in unrighteous thoughts and deeds. Christ took our sinful nature and destroyed it through His cross. He caused sin's influence to cease in our lives. Now we reckon ourselves dead to sin. Christ *has been* crucified, and when we put our trust in Him we *have been* crucified with Him. We can now consider ourselves victors over sin because we are in Him.

Many readers will say, "This sounds very good, but it is not what I observe in my life or the lives of others. The sinful nature continues to come to the surface, no matter how hard I fight it."

My response is, first, that part of the problem may be found in the fostering of a false understanding about salvation. When a person so often hears the teaching that sin is never finally dealt with in this life, she can learn to become resigned to an imperfect salvation. Many believe sin is inevitable, even in the life of the Christian, that we are both saved and sinner at the exact same time. This suggests that there is not a true present salvation, only a commitment to religion. It also suggests that Christ's work on the cross was not effective enough to completely deal with our present sinful state. Something is lacking in the power of the cross.

Did Christ save us fully and perfectly? The answer must certainly be yes. 1 John 1:9 says He not only forgave our sins but also cleansed us from all unrighteousness. Those who claim that Christ forgives sin but does not remove it must know that God was doing that very thing under the Old Testament sacrifices. That system could not do away with sin, only put a check on it. That covenant was not perfect enough, so He enacted a new covenant in the blood of Jesus (read Hebrews 7:18-22; 8:6; 10:1-18). Now Romans 8:1-4 declares, "Therefore, there is now no condemnation for those who are in Christ Jesus, because through Christ Jesus the law of the *Spirit* who gives life has *set you free from the law of sin* and death. *For what the law was powerless to do because it was weakened by the flesh, God did by sending his own Son in the likeness of sinful flesh to be a sin offering.* And so he condemned sin in the flesh, in order that the righteous requirement of the law might be fully met in us, who do not live according to the flesh but according to the Spirit."

We can think of sin in two forms. There are the sins we personally committed. These are the sins we asked forgiveness for when we came to Christ. But sin came into the world through Adam. That was his sin, yet as the federal head of the human race it affected all mankind. In Genesis 5:1-3 we are reminded that God created man in His own image, but after Adam sinned he began having children in his own image. This is the origin of the sinful nature. On the cross Jesus broke the power of sin over us, so that we would no longer be its slaves. He also has the power to cleanse our inner nature and make us new creations so we are reborn, not as children of Adam, but as children of God.

1 John 3:4-6 says, "Everyone who sins breaks the law; in fact, sin is lawlessness. But you know that he appeared so that he might take away our sins. And in him is no sin. No one who lives in him keeps on sinning. No one who continues to sin has either seen him or known him." 1 John 2:1 allows that sin might occur in an isolated sense, but the Greek tenses of 1 John 3 declare that those born of God cannot be characterized by habitual sin. John goes on to relate that Jesus came to destroy (literally, "to make of no effect") the devil (his power in our lives, which is the power of sin).

To live the lifestyle of the cross we must be united to Christ, who is dead to sin, and we must seek the power of the Holy Spirit, who enables us to be obedient.

To be crucified with Christ does not mean that we die for our sins, but that we accept the death of Christ, which was for the purpose of cleansing away our sins and cleansing us from all unrighteousness. We have become sharers in His death, and so sharers in His life.

We will always battle temptation. That is not sin. Jesus was tempted. But sin cannot rule us if God has delivered us from its power. When the Son sets us free, we are free indeed. Sin cannot lord it over us, unless we choose to allow it. Under the Old Testament law obedience was demanded and imperfection was condemned. The law could only deal with sin by punishing it. Then Jesus came to effectively satisfy the justice of God and to deal finally with the sinful human nature. We are not only commanded to obey, we are free and empowered to obey.

The message of Romans 6 is that both God and sin are looking for instruments for their use, and neither will share with the other. God has chosen to work through His people to accomplish many aspects of His redemptive purposes. Through His disciples He wants to demonstrate to the world what a community of love looks like. Sin also needs people in order to exist. The battle between righteousness and sin, God and Satan, is at work constantly, with the prize being human souls. We can't waver. We must choose our side. To be acceptable in God's sight is to abandon sin and any personal justification. To be in union with Christ is to have abandoned one kind of existence for another that Jesus has made possible. We must so totally identify ourselves by faith with the cross of Christ that it is the dominating power of our lives—the lifestyle of the cross.

Truly accepting Christ results in a definite change of life. Jesus didn't come to make us better. He came to make us new. The old is put to death. The new has come into existence by the power of God. It is a miracle! And it is all made evident in how we live and what we live for.

Being a Christian means more than that a moral change has taken place in one's life. It is a complete identification of one's life with the person and lordship of Jesus Christ. This results in a brand new value system and a brand new purpose. It is a real union with Christ, a sharing of His life and of His mind (1 Corinthians 2:16). It starts with a participation in His death that is wholly destructive to sin. It is fellowship in His resurrection. Ephesians 2:1-2,4-7 says, "As for you, you *were* dead in your transgressions and sins, in which you *used to* live when you followed the ways of this world. . . . But because of his great love for us, God, who is rich in mercy, made us alive with Christ even when we were dead in transgressions—it is by grace you have been saved. And God *raised us up with Christ* and seated us with him in the heavenly realms *in Christ Jesus.*"

Do we have to wait until we get to heaven in order to be really free from sin? God has already raised us up to heavenly places in Christ. That is our spiritual position. We are in Christ, the sinless One. Just as we cannot live our physical life if we are not in the air and the air is not in us, so we cannot live the life of God if we are not in Christ and Christ is not in us. We have been joined with Him in His death and resurrection when we accepted Him as Savior and Lord.

In order to live the lifestyle of the cross, one must be crucified with Christ by faith, becoming dead to sin so that one can become fully alive to God.

Chapter Eight

Not I, but Christ

The cross of Christ is the fullest expression of God's great grace. Part of the significance of the cross is that in it we find God's judgment on our human efforts to be right with Him. The fact that Jesus had to die on the cross to purchase our salvation tells us that our good works are not meritorious enough to satisfy God's standards and desires for our lives. Our morality is never sufficient. True righteousness is unattainable without outside help. Nothing we could ever accomplish on our own could earn us God's love or heaven. The gift of life is priceless. The good news is that God loves us, not because we deserve to be loved, but He loves us because He loves us. (Compare Deuteronomy 7:7-8, in which God tells the nation of Israel that He loves them, not because they are great or good, but because He loves them. In short, He loves them because He loves them.) We can never assign any other motivation to God's love. It is His nature and will to love us.

Another important fact is that none of us has the power to conquer the sinful nature. Sin is a slave-master from which we cannot free ourselves by our own power. This sinful nature causes a separation between us and a holy God, and we are helpless to remove it or change our nature by our own power. Nor do we have the capacity to neutralize sin's result—death. But Romans 5:6-8 declares hope. "You see, at just the right time, when we were still powerless, Christ died for the ungodly. Very rarely will anyone die for a righteous person, though for a good person someone might possibly dare to die. But God demonstrates his own love for us in this: While we were still sinners, Christ died for us."

We can do nothing good enough to merit God's love, favor, salvation, eternal life, or heaven. If we are to obtain these precious gifts, God Himself must intervene on our behalf and provide a way. The amazing news is that God did this in the person of His Son, Jesus Christ! He didn't have to do this. But He did. The cross is God's judgment on human effort to achieve spiritual goodness and eternal life, and at the same time, it is God's provision for us to realize these great gifts.

In Galatians 2:19-21, Paul claims, "For through the law I died to the law so that I might live for God. I have been crucified with Christ and I no longer live, but Christ lives in me. The life I now live in the body, I live by faith in the Son of God, who loved me and gave himself for me. I do not set aside the grace of God, for if righteousness could be gained through the law, Christ died for nothing!"

First, Paul declares that he has died to the law. He uses himself as an example of what is true of all believers. A careful reading of the passages in which Paul treats the old covenant law teaches us some important ways of perceiving the law. The law reveals principles of right and wrong, and so informs us of God's view of morality and justice. The law teaches us about our sinfulness; when we try to obey the law we discover that our sinful nature is in the way. In the old covenant law God made it plain that we are sinners in need of salvation, and no matter how much we try to keep the law we can never conquer our sinfulness and win salvation. The law makes us accountable for sin (Romans 5:13), but it cannot take away our sins. The law could only deal with sin by punishing it. Only the Lamb of God takes away the sins of the world, forgiving our sins and cleansing us from all unrighteousness (1 John 1:9). The law is the strength of sin because it makes us know our sinfulness and our helplessness to save ourselves. In 1 Corinthians 15:56 Paul wrote, "The sting of death is sin, and the power of sin is the law."

The law of Moses was given to put a check on sin until the Savior would come (Galatians 3:19-24). It required obedience, yet it was impossible to completely obey the law because of the human sinful nature. All have sinned, the Bible declares. The law demands obedience, but it provides no power to obey. It is a deterrent, but it does not bring salvation. It puts a restraint on sin, but could give no remedy for sin. The law could spell out the consequences of sin. The law demanded justice in the form of penalty for sin, but it could not change or remove the sinful nature. The law hopelessly condemns, since no one can fulfill its requirements. It offers no full salvation.

The law was also given to lead us to Christ (Galatians 3:24-25). It does us a great service in revealing to us our need for a Savior, and by foreshadowing the coming and ministry of that Savior. Christ is the end of the law (Romans 10:4), able to produce true righteousness in those who believe in Him. While the righteous demand of the law for sin was death, Christ fulfilled the law by His sinless life and death. In Christ we die to the law, the law's requirements having been satisfied in Him. He took the law's death penalty for us, and so, by having faith in His atoning work, our old nature has been crucified with Christ. As far as the law is concerned we have died. Then, because Christ lives, we enter upon a new life distinctly different in quality and kind from the old—eternal life.

When by faith we came to be *in Christ*, we shared in His crucifixion. We fellowshiped (participated in) His death. We died. Jesus did for us what the law could not do for us, and what we could not do for ourselves. Because we put our trust in Him, we experience in our own lives His death and His life.

Paul literally says, "With Christ I have been co-crucified." To be crucified to something means to die to it so that all relationship with it has ceased. In Romans 6:16 we read that Jesus died to sin. He had no sin, but He accomplished a death for our sin. In Galatians 2:20 we read that we have been crucified with Christ. Therefore, we also have died to sin, sharing by faith the very death of Jesus.

Paul also states that we have died to the law, meaning that the law no longer lays a penalty on us because our sins have been taken away. The death penalty of the law was satisfied by Jesus, and we partake of His death by faith. We have been justified (declared legally innocent) because of our faith in Christ's work. Additionally, our nature has been changed. Before we were sinners by nature, but we have been given a new nature; we have become a new creation.

What does all this mean? We are talking about Jesus' call for His disciples to live the lifestyle of the cross. We have heard the message of the cross and responded to it. Now Jesus also provides us with the means by which to live in accordance with all the cross has bought for us. When we realized that our effort to tame sin by trying to bring our sinful nature into line with an outward law was fruitless, and when we accepted the only means of salvation available to us (by God's grace), we died—died to sin, died to our good works (our ineffective efforts to be right with God through performance), and died to the law with all of its penalties. Christ became our source of righteousness. We are saved by faith in His grace. From that point of trusting faith that resulted in our justification (forgiveness of our sins), we can find power over sin. And as we surrender our redeemed selves up to God's lordship, we experience the heart-cleansing work of the Holy Spirit who renews our very nature and enables us to live obedient lives, not according to a law, but according to our new nature.

Salvation by personal merit brought frustration and further condemnation. But "there is now no condemnation for those who are in Christ Jesus, because through Christ Jesus the law of the Spirit who gives life has set you free from the law of sin and death. For what the law was powerless to do because it was weakened by the flesh, God did by sending his own Son in the likeness of sinful flesh to be a sin offering. And so he condemned sin in the flesh, in order that the righteous requirement of the law might be fully met in us, who do not live according to the flesh but according to the Spirit" (Romans 8:1-4).

We are not without a law, for there is the law of Christ, which is love (see Galatians 6:2 and Romans 13:8-10). The love of God poured into our hearts by the Holy Spirit (Romans 5:5) becomes the law that governs our actions, words, and motives. We live out that law because we are saved by grace through faith and have been given a nature after the likeness of Christ. We do not keep the law to get saved, but because we are saved. Many go to bookstores and try to find guidance about how to achieve personal wholeness through some kind of self-help behavior, only to discover that it is a futile enterprise. Our good works are not enough to achieve the life God intended. But after we have accepted salvation as a gift, our lives result naturally in the kind of good works that come from freedom from sin and selfishness. We obey, not to get saved, but because we have been saved.

Having spoken of this death to sin and the law, Paul's great claim in Galatians 2:20 is that Christ's life is lived out through him. This might be thought of as another kind of incarnation in which the resurrected Lord continues manifesting His life through His believers by dwelling within them. "I no longer live, but Christ lives in me." What a wonderful declaration! But what does it mean?

The way we died to the law was by being united by faith to Christ in His death on the cross. According to the Bible, if we have been united to Him in His death, we are also united with Him in His life. The old self of sin was crucified and the life we now live is literally the life of Christ, for He actually lives in and through us. This is not mere symbolism. This is real!

Jesus taught this same truth using the picture of a vine and its branches (John 15). He is the vine; we are the branches. The branches only live as long as they draw life from the vine. The vine's life is extended out through the branches. There is a vital and indispensable connection. Branches cannot live without the vine. And if for some reason the life of the vine ceases to flow into the branch, the branch dies and either drops off or is removed by the gardener. The branch has no life of its own. The branch literally lives the life of the vine. The vine sends its life into the branch.

The life we now live as Christians finds its source only and completely in Jesus. Our growth, vitality, and fruitfulness—all that involves our Christian life—must be appropriated by faith from Christ and is a gift from Christ. Without Him we are nothing.

There is no person in this universe who can live the Christian life. No one reading these pages has any power of his own to live the Christ-like life. Only one person has that power, and that is Jesus Christ Himself. Only Jesus has the power in Himself to perfectly live the righteous life that pleases the Father. But here is the good news: Jesus wants to live that life through us. It is certain that in our own strength we cannot do it. That is why, in order to be a Christian, we must be able to proclaim as Paul did: "I am not living this life. I have surrendered to Jesus Christ and He is living in me and through me. The life I now live is lived out moment by moment and in every aspect by faith in the Son of God." This requires radical surrender!

The life Paul is talking about is one in which Christ is given full sway over one's life. He is the Master. Jesus Himself made it plain that we cannot serve Him if we have any other masters besides Him. No other person or group of people, no other thing, no other interest or ambition, no occupation with yourself—Christ alone is Lord and Master. We do not live to ourselves, but to God. Self has died. It has been crucified with Christ. Having been united by faith to Him in death, we can truly share His resurrection life. The influence of the world's value system over us has ceased. We are freed from all other masters, internal and external. It is not I who live, but Christ who lives in me.

How many of us could make that claim? Do we dare? Do we believe that this is a possibility and not just an ideal? If it is merely an unreachable ideal, then we can excuse ourselves if we do not realize it. But if it is indeed an unreachable ideal, then Paul's claim is negated, because he claimed to be experiencing it. And if we negate Paul's claim in this one thing, we bring other teachings of his into doubt. Was Paul telling the truth when he said he had been crucified with Christ and it was no longer he who lived but Christ in him? If he was telling the truth, then it is possible for all believers.

I urge the reader to finish this volume. Read every Scripture text I cite in its context. Study them for yourself and judge whether the Bible teaches complete salvation from sin and self and the perfect efficacy of the cross of Christ. If the Bible does teach these things, pray to God that you will be able to live the lifestyle of the cross! Plunge fully into the Christ-centered, Holy

Spirit–powered, purposeful, abundant, fruitful life Christ died in order for you to live. Do not take Christ's name and then make His suffering in vain in your life. Accept nothing less than the full benefits of His shed blood in your soul. We must judge our experience by Scripture; we must not judge Scripture by our experience. In other words, to say "I can never obtain that standard, therefore the Bible must not mean that," is to judge Scripture by our experience. To say, "The Bible teaches this and I have not attained to it, meaning I must complete my surrender to Christ," is to allow Scripture to dictate what our experience needs to be.

We can claim all of this by faith, but true faith is active, not passive. The following things will be true of a life in which true faith is at work.

First, Jesus is allowed full priority and lordship.

Second, the life we now live is not the result of our successful efforts to be righteous, but rather a result of trusting Christ. We rest now in the victories Christ has won for us. We are not merely looking to some future victory over sin. Christ has conquered, and we can believe it and go about the task of living knowing that sin need no longer be a constant hindrance. We cannot be successful living the Christian life by our power, struggling without victory over things that still bind us. Believe in the fullness of Christ's salvation and be set free. If you believe that you cannot have victory over sin, and that somehow Christ's cross is not sufficient to deal finally with your old self, you will continue to live in the belief that freedom is not possible in this life— and that will be exactly what you experience. Think about this: Christ is sinless. He cannot live in you if you continue to sin as a pattern of life. His living in you is evidence of His victory over sin for you.

Third, your interests are no longer your own. Your first desire is to fulfill the will of God.

Fourth, your life is no longer your own; you belong to Christ. You are one with Christ. My life is His. His life is mine. He has put His Spirit, His mind, His love, His joy, His peace, and His righteousness within me so that we are joined. His purpose is now my purpose. In fact, the only person who truly possesses eternal life is God, for He alone is eternal and He alone possesses the principle of life underived from any other sources. Therefore, when the Bible tells us that we have eternal life, it must necessarily be the very life of God, His kind and quality of life shared with us.

When we begin to live according to our own strength and when our interests conflict with those of God, we will experience the consequences of having moved out of the center of His will. Those consequences include confusion, weakness, and guilt.

Fifth, the motivating principle of your life will be specific. You will not be governed by a set of carnal rules to keep you from sinning, but by faith in the Son of God who in His love freed you from your sinful nature. We no longer have to sin. It is not inevitable. We no longer need feel condemned. To yet cling to your own efforts to be right with God, to attempt to tame sin by our own power, is to side-step the sufficient power of God's grace.

God does expect us to do what is right, but not in order to win His love (He loved us even when we were yet sinners), but rather because we love Him. Obedience to God is the evidence of our love for Him (John 14:15). Salvation gives us the power to do good, to be good. Good works are not a way to obtain salvation, or even maintain it. Rather, good works are the natural fruit and evidence of a saved and changed life.

We still live in a human body, but we live in this body by faith in the Son of God who loves us and gave Himself up for us to fully save us from the evil power of sin. That faith joins us to Christ in His death and in His life. We no longer live, but Christ lives in us—and through us.

Chapter Nine

Crucified in Weakness, Living in Power

*I*n time of trial and trouble we are especially aware of our weakness. In unavoidable situations we are sometimes bogged down, discouraged, or frustrated by our lack of control over circumstances. These times come, and when they do our first response should be to go to God in trusting prayer. Even though we may be aware of our weakness we must never lose sight of God's strength. 2 Corinthians 13:4 says, "For to be sure, he [Christ] was crucified in weakness, yet he lives by God's power. Likewise, we are weak in him, yet by God's power we will live with him in our dealing with you."

Reading this verse in context we discover that Paul is dealing with the issue of his apostolic authority. Because of Paul's gentleness and meekness there were some in the Corinthian church who tried to cast doubt on his authority. But Paul reminded them that Jesus also was gentle and meek. He did not exercise His authority to save Himself; rather, He was crucified in weakness. This appeared to many at that time to be the ultimate indication of Jesus' lack of power. But Jesus was not powerless. He voluntarily laid down

His life for us. And now He lives by the power of God. He was raised to glory at the right hand of the Father, and there, in divine power, He exercises all authority in heaven and earth (Matthew 28:18). Paul reminded the Corinthian believers that, though he himself may appear weak to them, that same power of God is active in him to deal with them.

Christ is powerful in the genuine Christian's life and personality. Paul appeared powerless to some because he exercised his power in gentleness instead of harshness. But though he appeared weak, he was fully aware of the power of God working in him.

An excellent definition of the biblical term "meekness" is "great power under control and reserved for sacred purposes." A person who possesses this type of meekness walks with confidence and without the need to vindicate himself, because he is aware of the power of God within him always ready to be called upon at the right time and for the right purpose.

The power of Christ is powerful in all of His true people to give them authority to stand against the spiritual foe. It is powerful to enable us to live as obedient Christians. And it is powerful to make us effective witnesses. But, unlike Paul, many of us, though professing our belief in God's power, have little confidence that it will work through us, and so we exercise little authority over darkness. Our belief in that power at work within us is theological, but we do not always believe for practical results. We have not really come to accept that we *can* do all things through Christ who strengthens us. And so many Christians go on not only in apparent weakness, but in actual weakness.

We are weak, but God is strong. And it is no longer I who live, but Christ who lives in me (Galatians 2:20). Christ can be actively and actually mighty in and through my life. Consider Paul's words in Ephesians 1:18-20: "I pray that the eyes of your heart may be enlightened in order that you may know the hope to which he has called you, the riches of his glorious inheritance in his holy people, and *his incomparably great power for us who believe. That power is the same as the mighty strength he exerted when he raised Christ from the dead* and seated him at his right hand in the heavenly realms." The power that is available to Jesus' disciples is the same power that raised Him from the dead. The Christian life—the lifestyle of the cross—is lived in resurrection power! If we have died with Him, we live in Him.

Paul continued in Ephesians 3:17-21: "And I pray that you, being rooted and established in love, *may have power, together with all the Lord's holy people*, to grasp how wide and long and high and deep is the love of Christ, and to know this love that surpasses knowledge—*that you may be filled to the measure of all the fullness of God.* Now to him who is able to do immeasurably more than all we ask or imagine, *according to his power that is at work within us*, to him be glory in the church and in Christ Jesus throughout all generations, for ever and ever! Amen."

If we have been crucified with Christ, joining Him in His death by faith, then we are alive now, being joined to Him by faith in His life. If Christ was crucified in weakness, so were we. And if Christ now lives by the power of God, so do we. Through the Holy Spirit, Christ wants to produce the effects of His death and resurrection in our lives as we fully identify with Jesus by faith. Our relationship with Christ is one of *union*. Not our power, but God's power, is active in us.

And yet, we have a tendency to look at our own strength only and thereby put a limit on what God can do in and through us. The lifestyle of the cross is resurrection living! The lifestyle of the cross is living believing all things are possible for those who believe. Life is full of possibilities that would not be humanly possible. God is able to do more than we can think or imagine according to His power at work in us!

In Matthew 17:20 Jesus said, "Nothing will be impossible for you." How can this be? We cannot put that kind of faith in ourselves. We are not almighty. Neither is it enough to put faith in faith ("if you had more faith you could do this"). Jesus' words can only be realized by having faith in God. In Matthew 19:26 Jesus said, "With man this is impossible, but with God all things are possible." It is by nothing less than the power of God that the lifestyle of the cross can be lived. We cannot do it. But we have died to self and live for God. It is no longer I who live but Christ who lives through me.

God's church puts many limitations on itself. God's people individually put limits on what God can do in and through them. Jesus' disciples have been given power over snakes and scorpions. They have power to do the will of God. They have power to speak the truth. Christ is the Head of the church and His life goes out through every member.

We look at our potential through temporal eyes of doubt and sense. Am I really able to bring people to Christ? We're thinking of what we can do alone, not with Christ. We are weak, but He is strong. And He lives in and through us.

The outcome of our limited perception is that we don't witness. We don't give. We don't build up the church. We don't make a difference. Our great talent is to list what we cannot do. Our efforts to pray, heal, and witness are often halfhearted, done with the expectation of limited results. We apply this criteria to what we do and what we think we can be.

I once heard a story about how circus elephants are tamed. When the elephant is very young it is fastened by a heavy chain and manacle around its ankle and the chain is attached to a heavy stake driven into the ground. The elephant is bound in such a way that its movements are very limited. Later on, the chain is replaced by a small rope tied to a wooden peg in the ground. However, by this time the elephant has learned to believe that his range of motion is limited. The mighty adult elephant is prevented from running away, not by the strength of the rope, but by the power of what it believes. But if a fire occurs, the elephant will be thrown into a panic and pull at the rope. Having discovered that it really can move, no one will ever again be able to limit that elephant with a mere rope.

When we are given freedom by Christ, we might at first have trouble believing in its full extent. What does it take to cause us to begin to move in God's strength? The tent is burning around us! The world of people around us is in danger. Destruction is immanent. We don't want to run away. We want to rescue some. But first we must discover how free we are to move in the power of God.

Let us get a vision of the urgency of the work God has given us. Let us shake off our perceived limitations. God is almighty. We can live and serve and obey confidently. Like Peter who began to doubt and sink into the waves, we flounder when we only consider what we can do. But the church should be about doing what can only be done by the strength of God.

We are weak, but Christ is strong. We are joined with Him; He was crucified in weakness and lives in power. Paul declared in Ephesians 6:10, "Finally, be strong in the Lord and in his mighty power." Strong—in the Lord. We are not weak in the Lord.

Do you know that Christ is in you (2 Corinthians 13:5)? In Philippians 4:13 Paul declared, "I can do all things through him [Christ] who gives me strength." The lifestyle of the cross may sometimes involve suffering for Christ's sake, but it is also characterized by victory and power. By faith in our all-powerful Lord we can do all things according to His revealed will and for

His glory. We can do powerful things for the proclamation of the gospel, the deliverance and healing of lives, the edification of the church, and the increase of the kingdom of God in the world. Certainly there are those circumstances that remind us of our weakness, but Jesus is the Lord of all situations. We are enabled to live above sin, have hope in tragedy, overcome paralyzing fears, and endure trials as we live for God—all because we are united with the life of Christ by faith.

God loves you and is not stingy with His power. Commit all to Him. Be His follower. Exercise authority over Satan. Demonstrate the power of love. Do not limit what God can do in your life and through your life. If we have been crucified with Christ in weakness, we live in His resurrection power unto new life.

Chapter Ten

The Difference Is the Cross

You have probably heard the saying among church folk, "In the world but not of it." Those words are based on Jesus' prayer to the Father in John 17:14-16: "They are not of the world any more than I am of the world. My prayer is not that you take them out of the world but that you protect them from the evil one. They are not of the world, even as I am not of it." "In the world but not of the world" is a true saying, but it is also something we can say very easily, whether or not we intend to live up to it.

What is the real difference between the disciples of Jesus and the world? Is there something we can really lay our finger on, something beyond mere moral beliefs, religious rituals, or church tradition? When we say we are a "peculiar people" (1 Peter 2:9, KJV), what is that specific thing to which we would direct the world's attention? What is the proof that we are not merely another group devoted religiously to good morals and a particular worldview? If we claim to be a changed people, what kind of change are we talking about, and how did the change happen? What is the difference, really?

There are many passages of Scripture that could be used to talk about the distinctives of Christianity, but our study in this chapter will focus on a few verses in 1 Peter 4:1-6: "Therefore, since Christ suffered in his body, arm yourselves also with the same attitude, because whoever suffers in the body is done with sin. As a result, they do not live the rest of their earthly lives for evil human desires, but rather for the will of God. For you have spent enough time in the past doing what pagans choose to do—living in debauchery, lust, drunkenness, orgies, carousing and detestable idolatry. They are surprised that you do not join them in their reckless, wild living, and they heap abuse on you. But they will have to give account to him who is ready to judge the living and the dead. For this is the reason the gospel was preached even to those who are now dead, so that they might be judged according to human standards in regard to the body, but live according to God in regard to the spirit."

Let us first try to answer in a general way the question of what makes us truly different. Peter wrote much about suffering for the right. However, we are not different because we have some sort of a martyr's attitude. Peter wrote that the world is surprised because we do not join in doing the same things they are doing. Our lives have been changed from occupation with such things to occupation with something else. Our pattern of thinking has been transformed, our values changed, our priorities reoriented, our desires refocused. Our very purpose in life is different since we met Christ. We have a new quality of life. The world is shocked because we have left certain things behind for something they do not understand. They are controlled by fleshly lusts and desires. But for us, Romans 12:2 is a reality: "Do not conform to the pattern of this world, but be transformed by the renewing of your mind. Then you will be able to test and approve what God's will is—his good, pleasing and perfect will."

The differences between us and those living by the world's value system should be obvious. Let us turn our attention to the focal point of the Christian experience of conversion from death to life. That crisis point is what makes the real difference.

The distinction between the followers of Christ and the followers of the world's value system is manifest in matters of morality, yet the difference itself is not mere morality. The difference is one thing—the cross of Christ! Christianity is moral, but mere morality is not Christianity. The Christian life is more than a matter of the individual's sinful activity being curtailed. It is a matter of personal sin being forgiven (justification) and it is a matter of the inner nature itself being cleansed and changed (holiness). It is a matter of the removal of all the barriers that exist in our own nature to a personal relationship with God.

To be a Christian does not mean that we have endeavored, by our own will power, to be moral against our inner impulses. In Christ, the very nature of our inner impulses is changed. It is the cross that makes us different. We believe in the perfect effectiveness of the cross of Christ to deliver us from the guilt consequential to the sins we have committed, and to deliver us even from the bent to sin (the sinful nature) that causes all of Adam's children to fall short of the glory of God. We have been both forgiven and purified of all unrighteousness (1 John 1:9). We are both pardoned for our past and empowered to be obedient now. In completely identifying with Christ by faith and being joined in union with Him through the power of His Spirit, we become armed with the same mind of Christ to follow the way of the cross. Having been crucified with Him we have died to the sin in which we walked. *The cross is the difference.*

The reason that we do not walk as the world walks is not that we have succeeded in making ourselves righteous, or that we have stronger will power than others, or that we were born into this world better than others, but because our sinful nature has been crucified with Christ and we have been made new creations in Christ. The grace of God manifest in the cross of Christ is the only point of difference. The cross alone is the reason we are in the world but not of the world. The cross has affected our separation from the world and our reconciliation with God.

I repeat, even though Christianity is moral, morality alone is not Christianity. Many are confused at this point. Nor is Christianity to be equated with humanitarianism or philanthropy. It is not our efforts to be different that make us different. Rather it is the fact that we trust in Christ who was crucified and is now alive. We participate in His death and in His life by faith, and that faith is more than the use of imagination to generate a hoped-for reality. It is our trust placed in something real, thus inviting God to impart a new kind of life that is genuine and effective.

It is the cross that makes the difference. It makes us different from the world because it makes us different from what we once were. We cannot take the credit for the change. It was Christ who was sacrificed. Our salvation is accomplished by nothing but the grace of God through Jesus. When He called us to decide to accept Him as our Savior and surrender to Him as Lord, He responded as promised with the free gift of eternal life, which includes the power to live that special kind of life.

Peter said that the world is surprised that we do not join them in appeasing the flesh. They are shocked at our strangeness. 1 Peter 4:4 says, "They are surprised that you do not join them in their reckless, wild living, and they heap abuse on you." In fact, our new God-given values are irreconcilably different from the world's values.

Many identify Christian values with the traditional Western lifestyle (at least before recent wide-ranging changes in American moral values). Many American individuals and groups work to protect human and civil rights, yet they by-pass biblical teachings about right and wrong. Some choices in the moral arena are defended under the heading of civil or human rights but God's Word forbids them. Clearly, the world's definition of justice does not always agree with the idea of justice or rights in the context of the kingdom of Jesus. Modern day thought holds that each individual is accountable to his own individual sense of right and wrong. This is even changing the nature of civil laws. Absolute standards are refused, and when that happens civil laws are in danger of becoming merely a set of expediencies agreed upon by whoever happens to be in power at the time. Human dignity is not preserved under those conditions.

Jesus' followers live their lives according to a set of values that this world sometimes adopts in part (when it results in their personal protection), but which we adopt in full, oftentimes at the displeasure of the world. Peter's words are an exhortation to be separated from ungodliness, and our motivation is our realization of what the cross of Christ is all about. We are not motivated by a desire just to be the best religion or to be better than everybody else. We are moved by the love God has shown to us, what Jesus did for our sakes. And we are motivated by the love with which we love God in return. The cross is God's unarguable demonstration of His unreserved love for a guilty world, a world we have been a part of. What amazing love! If human love motivates us, divine love compels us. Because Christ suffered, we "arm ourselves" with the same mind—to undergo anything for the service of our Lord and Savior (see 1 Peter 4:1; see also Philippians 2:5-8).

The cross of Christ is the only thing that separates us from the world. It is the historical truth event that informs our values, feelings, and goals. It is the cross that teaches us what we know about real love. It is the cross that shows us the way to be made free from sin. It is the cross of Christ that reveals to us, as nothing else can, the heart of God Himself toward us.

Chapter Eleven

Sharing the Sufferings

In a previous chapter, we learned that when we speak of the cross of Christ, and so also of the cross He commanded us to carry, we cannot omit the meanings of suffering and sacrifice for the accomplishment of God's redemptive will in the world without diluting the message of the cross. The positive message of the cross is that it is the power to save, but that victory was accomplished by sacrifice. We must do nothing to empty the cross of the power to save, and that means we cannot always make the message of the cross pleasing to sinners, because on the cross Jesus condemned sin. The cross must continue to speak, as it did at first, of the sinfulness of man and his need to repent, of the deadly wages of sin, and then of God's mercy toward every person in sending His Son to die in our place that we might be saved. The cross represents grace—Christ taking upon Himself what each of us deserved.

Therefore, let us consider further this idea of suffering that is inextricably a part of the meaning of Christ's cross, and therefore part of the meaning of the lifestyle of the cross Jesus calls upon His followers to live.

In 1 Peter 4:1 we read, "Therefore, since Christ suffered in his body, arm yourselves also with the same attitude." We are called upon to take on the same manner of thinking as Christ. We are to share the same intent and resolution to suffer in the flesh that Christ had. Doing God's will is joyous, but it may also lead to suffering. Jesus is our pattern in this suffering as much as in power and victory.

Peter continues in the same verse: "because whoever suffers in the body is done with sin." What does he mean by this? It involves at least this: one would not willingly suffer for the right unless he or she had been delivered from sin. If a person can come through persecution that might be the result of living for Christ without denying Christ or compromising with the world, that person is obviously "done with sin" and devoted to the truth at any cost to self.

The one who has shared the suffering and death of Christ is risen to a life in which sin no longer has control. Such a person voluntarily and with clear understanding comes over from worldliness to Christ, coming to that position through the cross (death to sin) to the power of the resurrection (new life in Christ). Such a person is identified with Christ (including both suffering and His resurrection life), not only in regards to her initial conversion, but in regards to all life on an ongoing basis. She represents the good ground in which the seed grows and bears fruit in contrast to the types of ground that forbid or arrest such growth and fruit. In participating in both the death and life of Christ by faith in union with Him, we share His victory over the power of sin, the sting of death, and the value system of the world.

Peter admonishes us to "arm" ourselves "also with the same attitude" as Christ who suffered in His body. Christ's suffering had redemptive purpose, and in our participation in His redemptive purpose in the world, we are liable to experience rejection. Believers are to adopt Christ's way of thinking that takes into account and accepts the risks of walking in God's will and standing for God's values. Philippians 2:5 says, "Have the same mindset as Christ Jesus," and then goes on to describe Jesus' willingness to subject Himself to the sort of servanthood to God for the sake of men that resulted in His obedience to God, even to death on the cross.

Now, the Bible does not advocate a martyr complex. I once knew a woman who took Jesus' prediction that the world would hate His disciples to mean that the more people disliked her, the more righteous she was. That included not only unbelievers but church folk as well. So, she went about being difficult to people, declaring her beliefs even in the church in ways that would rub people the wrong way in an apparent attempt to insure her righteousness as reflected in rejection. She actually seemed to be offended when people returned her obnoxious attitude with patience and kindness. If the world does not like us it must be because our message and our lives prick their conscience and not because we are obnoxious. The Bible does tell us that we must be united to the suffering of Christ. We must be ready for the gospel's sake to undergo suffering. We must not compromise for the sake of being acceptable to the world. But neither do we deliberately provoke hard feelings just to prove we are right by martyrdom. Remember, false religions have suffering martyrs and that does not prove them to be right.

Romans 8:16-17 says, "The Spirit himself testifies with our spirit that we are God's children. Now if we are children, then we are heirs—heirs of God and co-heirs with Christ, *if indeed we share in his sufferings in order that we may also share in his glory.*" Notice the "if." Sharing in Christ's glory is conditional on our sharing in His suffering.

Hebrews 13:12-13 reads, "And so Jesus also suffered outside the city gate to make the people holy through his own blood. Let us, then, go to him outside the camp, bearing the disgrace he bore." The phrase "outside the camp" suggests the exclusion the world will often force upon us. We want to be loving and friendly, but our message will also bring to us the rejection of a world that insists on not being under conviction for the sins it wants to allow. The world determines that sin will be the norm. Our message, in words and deeds, declares there is a wonderful life lived according to a wholly different value system—but it requires renouncing sin.

The words of Paul in Philippians 3:8-11 read, "What is more, I consider everything a loss because of the surpassing worth of knowing Christ Jesus my Lord, for whose sake I have lost all things. I consider them garbage, that I may gain Christ and be found in him, not having a righteousness of my own that comes from the law, but that which is through faith in Christ—the righteousness that comes from God on the basis of faith. I want to know Christ—yes, to know the power of his resurrection and *participation in his sufferings, becoming like him in his death, and so, somehow, attaining to the resurrection from the dead."* Note again the conditionality of this promise: attaining to the resurrection involves fellowshipping (participating in) Christ's sufferings, becoming like Him in His death (to sin and worldliness). For Christ the way to the resurrection was through suffering and death. So to live the life of a disciple we must die a death to sin and live this life out in this world—the lifestyle of the cross. The way to the glory of resurrection life in the future and resurrection living in the present is through death to sin and a willingness to suffer, if need be, in the world for Jesus' name.

Every one of these Scripture passages expresses the truth that we must participate in (Greek *koinonia*, to share in, fellowship) the suffering of Christ in order to participate in His life. We are to do God's good will in a world bent on evil. Jesus declared in the Sermon on the Mount that those who are persecuted for His sake will be blessed. Those who save their lives (physical, material, social) will lose them.

Someone might say that the Christians of the early church were being persecuted by the Roman government and this is the reason Paul and Peter wrote in this way, and we who live in a free society don't have to take these words so literally. We know there are places in the world where Christians are suffering greatly and dying for their faith, but not here. First, remember that Paul wrote in 1 Corinthians that we are all members of one body and when one member of the body suffers the whole body is suffering. Second, do not be deceived. Sin is sin everywhere. Even in a civilized and free society, sinners will reject, be offended by, and even persecute true believers. We will be called upon to make choices. Recall Paul's words in 2 Timothy 3:12: "Everyone who wants to live a godly life in Christ Jesus will be persecuted."

The world today is no less sinful or apt to scoff at God than the world of ancient times. And the church today is not less accountable for its commitment to please God. Let us not allow our freedom in one place to lead us into thinking the way of God and the way of the world have come to friendly terms over time. Is the need for the gospel message, in word and deed, any less urgent? Can the church settle down into its buildings and pews and consider the job basically done? Is the message of the cross any less offensive to a sin-bent world? Is the message any less powerful?

In 2 Timothy 1:8-9 Paul wrote, "So do not be ashamed of the testimony about our Lord or of me his prisoner. Rather, join with me in suffering for the gospel, by the power of God. He has saved us and called us to a holy life." Is it shame or embarrassment that keeps us from speaking to those around us? Has the world succeeded in convincing us that our values and message are out of date? Many Christians today are not willing to carry the cross, to suffer for the gospel. We may not be called upon to suffer torture or martyrdom, but the suffering may come in the form of rejection, mocking, exclusion, inconvenience, and so forth. Are we too often in self-preservation mode rather than trusting God to watch over us in our obedience? Must we accommodate the attitudes of the world to keep from feeling uncomfortable in the world? Can we always remember that while we are citizens of this planet, we are first of all citizens of the kingdom of God?

Look at the following examples from the Bible. Acts 5:40-42 relates, "They called the apostles in and had them flogged. Then they ordered them not to speak in the name of Jesus, and let them go. The apostles left the Sanhedrin, rejoicing because they had been counted worthy of suffering disgrace for the Name. Day after day, in the temple courts and from house to house, they never stopped teaching and proclaiming the good news that Jesus is the Messiah." We avoid witnessing for far less reasons of inconvenience than those experienced by these early believers.

1 Peter 2:21 says, "To this you were called, because Christ suffered for you, leaving you an example, that you should follow in his steps."

1 Peter 4:12-16 says, "Dear friends, do not be surprised at the fiery ordeal that has come on you to test you, as though something strange were happening to you. But rejoice inasmuch as you *participate in the sufferings of Christ, so that* you may be overjoyed when his glory is revealed. If you are insulted because of the name of Christ, you are blessed, for the Spirit of glory and of God rests on you. If you suffer, it should not be as a murderer or thief or any other kind of criminal, or even as a meddler. However, if you suffer as a Christian, do not be ashamed, but praise God that you bear that name."

The church on earth is characterized by endurance and courage (see Romans 5:3-5). It does not grow weak in its commitment to be all God wills. Let the church be the church in times like these. The disciples whose experiences are described in these texts considered it joy to suffer for Christ, not that suffering is joyful, but the joy of knowing Christ made suffering purposeful.

The cross and the fullness of its meanings permeate every aspect of a true Christian way of life. It was on the cross that Jesus bought our salvation. It remains central, not just historically, but presently. We have been commanded to carry our cross as the way to follow Christ. It is the cross that distinguishes God's people from the world and from any other religion, for the cross dealt finally and sufficiently with our sinful nature and radically changed our lives. By faith we are united to Christ in His suffering and death, and so also in His newness of powerful life. Anyone who has not participated in His suffering through complete identification through faith in His work on the cross and commitment to His lordship in this life cannot experience His life (see Romans 8:16-17). The only way to live the resurrection life is to experience selfless death.

In this chapter I have spoken of the need for disciples of Jesus to be willing to suffer for the redemptive purpose of God in the world—living the life and sharing the message given meaning by the cross of Christ. We have read the words of Peter and others who asserted that fleshly desires are fruits of the world's value system, which believers are to reject in their identification with the passionate suffering of the Savior for the sins of the world. We are no longer set on pleasing ourselves, but God. If all of these things are true and we are indeed willing to risk everything for the knowledge of Christ, we will bear fruit. Believers and churches that do not bear fruit have not yet attained or committed to the lifestyle of the cross that Jesus requires of His disciples.

In Matthew 3:8, John the baptizer said, "Produce fruit in keeping with repentance." To repent means literally to "change one's mind." We have changed our minds about sin and about God. The only Lord over us is Jesus Christ. This will be evidenced in our way of life and what our life produces. It is manifest that we have left the life of sin behind and devoted ourselves unreservedly to loving God. This fruit is to be borne in all of our concerns, relationships, purposes, decisions, and attitudes. This is the life of holiness made possible by the cross and resurrection and empowered by the indwelling of the Holy Spirit.

Dear reader, is Christ the focal point of all your life? Are you fully committed to bearing fruit to Him by the power of the indwelling Spirit received in complete surrender of your will? Are you bearing fruit that demonstrates that you have been made different from the world in your values and goals? Are you willing to take the message of the cross of Christ to others, to live it before others, regardless of what the world thinks? We do not deliberately seek suffering, but we do not fear it either if we know that it is a participation in the suffering of Him who suffered for us as we take the message of God's love and salvation to all who will receive it, and with a view of the glory of the Redeemer we will share in eternity.

Do we fear suffering? It is only natural. No one cherishes pain. But our God is great, and this life is temporary. Paul said in Romans 8:18, "I consider that our present sufferings are not worth comparing with the glory that will be revealed in us." Christ must take priority over anything in this life. We will all stand before Him someday, and the things of this world will have passed away.

What kind of church does Christ seek to build where you are? If we are satisfied with merely keeping a building and making sure a group meets there every Sunday, we can have that. What is the measure of effectiveness for a congregation of the church? But if we are interested in doing the will of God that Jesus did and wants to continue through us, we must move beyond the walls of the building. Let that be a nurturing place where we gather to worship, to learn and to be encouraged. But then let us make the world around us the great context for living the lifestyle of the cross and communicating the message of the cross in all our daily interactions. Let us sacrifice ourselves to this redemptive work God wants to use our lives to promote. And because our mission field is a world hostile to God, let us not be surprised at the trials we experience, but let us rejoice that we are deemed worthy to suffer for the name of Christ and for the winning of lives for Christ.

I once heard a minister ask his congregation this question: "If you got up this morning and this church had disappeared, what effect would its absence have on the community?" Then he said, "If no effect, then this church should disappear, for it is unnecessary." God needs every voice for the truth. Let's not fade into the background of the culture, but rather let us change the culture with an ever-new and renewing message. There is new life in Christ!

What concerns God is that souls are dying every day and going into eternity not knowing Him. But God has left a people with a message to speak and live that has the power to change the lives of others. He wants us to live and speak with a sense of urgency for those dying souls. Sharing the suffering means being willing to risk the pain in order to love people and make known God's truth. This will require putting temporal concerns in their proper place, and even sacrificing them at times. But no suffering we are allowed to go through for God while we live for Him on this earth can compare with that of a soul suffering hell forever. Christ died on the cross to make a difference. Carrying our cross means making a difference. What difference will you make?

Chapter Twelve

Some Perspective on Suffering for Christ

The Bible tells us that the spirit of antichrist is already an active influence in the world (1 John 2:18). This spirit is directed against God's kingdom by seducing human hearts away from Christ and the true message of the cross. This is often done by presenting a counterfeit Christian message. The prefix "anti" in Greek means "instead of." "Antichrist" is any person or influence that sets itself up in place of Christ. The spirit of antichrist creates a false or counterfeit spiritual condition that represents itself as genuine Christianity, but it is not. This counterfeit can include a form of the church that represents itself as the church but does not present the New Testament picture of the church. When examined in the light of Scripture this form of church does not meet the standard. There are always problems in every congregation, and every small and large group must always be seeking to be what God wills. But to do that they must examine the Scriptures. Too often we resort to our own preferences. The church is of God, but there are various man-made inventions that do not meet the divine criteria of the church of God. The church must not judge itself successful because it is busy, but rather it must always consider whether it is fulfilling Christ's commission.

In Chapter 6 we saw that some preach a different Jesus, a different gospel, and a different spirit (2 Corinthians 11:4). These are counterfeit forms and produce a counterfeit church. The world accepts these counterfeit forms of the church because they claim to be the church. Thus, the world forms its opinion of what the church is. To expound on this would require another book. The cure is the undiluted message of the cross informing each believer and body of believers what they are to be.

We often think of "antichrist" as a persecuting power, but one of the ways this spirit of antichrist influences the Christian church is by soothing it into a state of comfort, inactivity, and satisfaction with the cultural and institutional status quo in the church. The spirit of antichrist tries to substitute something with the appearance of truth for that which is of God, including our lifestyle and our message. The spirit of antichrist desires to thwart Christ's ministry in the world, a ministry that God wants to accomplish through the church. This is why the spirit of antichrist especially directs its efforts to distort the church from within. We think of persecution as coming from outside the church, but it can happen within the church through strife and factions. More insidious still, the church falls under the spell of thinking a certain way about the church that isn't always biblical—however, it may be more comfortable than really being the church (review Chapter 11).

Sometimes this spirit of complacency (compare Amos 6:1) is evident among the followers of Christ. The church (whether a congregation or the church in general influenced by the surrounding culture) develops an unwillingness to risk social disapproval and puts much effort into gaining such approval. (Note: there are church groups who have brought upon themselves social disapproval that is deserved, but they usually have the disapproval of many other believers as well.) There are many exceptions, for there are many believers and congregations who understand and live out what the church is all about. But much of the church in America and in the rest of the world is in a state of cultural infiltration that weakens it in the carrying out of a real fruit-bearing mission. If we are going to be ambassadors of Christ in a sinful world, will not some conflict be inevitable (2 Timothy 3:12)? When spiritual light shines in spiritual darkness, the darkness does not give way easily.

Our primary text for this chapter is 2 Corinthians 4:7–5:1: "But we have this treasure in jars of clay to show that this all-surpassing power is from God and not from us. We are hard pressed on every side, but not crushed; perplexed, but not in despair; persecuted, but not abandoned; struck down, but not destroyed. We always carry around in our body the death of Jesus, so that the life of Jesus may also be revealed in our body. For we who are alive are always being given over to death for Jesus' sake, so that his life may be revealed in our mortal body. So then, death is at work in us, but life is at work in you.

"It is written: 'I believed; therefore I have spoken.' Since we have that same spirit of faith, we also believe and therefore speak, because we know that the one who raised the Lord Jesus from the dead will also raise us with Jesus and present us with you to himself. All this is for your benefit, so that the grace that is reaching more and more people may cause thanksgiving to overflow to the glory of God.

"Therefore we do not lose heart. Though outwardly we are wasting away, yet inwardly we are being renewed day by day. For our light and momentary troubles are achieving for us an eternal glory that far outweighs them all. So we fix our eyes not on what is seen, but on what is unseen, since what is seen is temporary, but what is unseen is eternal.

"For we know that if the earthly tent we live in is destroyed, we have a building from God, an eternal house in heaven, not built by human hands."

The first point made in this passage is that there is *power in weakness*. Moral weakness is not a position of power. Paul is thinking about the fact that we are made from the dust of the earth. Paul uses the descriptive phrase "jars of clay." This has to do with our frailty and finiteness. Mankind, for all the power and glory he might attribute to his intellectual and technical accomplishments, is still characteristically weak. We find ourselves frequently subject to circumstances beyond our control. We are liable to error, illness, and addiction. We are mortal. We are, as Abraham stated in Genesis 18, but dust and ashes.

Yet, for Christians, a wonderful privilege has been bestowed on us by God's grace. We, though containers of clay, have been filled with God's Spirit and power. We are still clay, but we are now containers of priceless treasure. Verse 6 says that God "made his light shine in our hearts to give us the light of the knowledge of God's glory displayed in the face of Christ." In other words, we have been given the greatest treasure of all, the gospel message, to fill us and give us purpose to share. This gospel is not just in the form of words, but comes with the Giver of those words. The Spirit of Christ Himself has written the gospel on our hearts, made it an internal part of our nature, and continues to energize us through the gospel by His constant presence in our surrendered hearts.

We may observe much infirmity in our earthly life, but God has given much glory to our lives as well. However, we must always remember that the weakness is ours, and the glory is God's. We must never come to think that God cannot do without us, or that it is in any way possible to do the work of God in our own power and wisdom. Nor should we think that God is unable to do anything through us because we are inadequate. God told Paul at a time when the apostle was going through a period of suffering, "My grace is sufficient for you, for my power is made perfect in weakness." Paul responded, "Therefore I will boast all the more gladly about my weakness, so that Christ's power may rest on me. That is why, for Christ's sake, I delight in weakness, in insults, in hardships, in persecutions, in difficulties. For when I am weak, then I am strong" (2 Corinthians 12:9-10).

When we admit our dependence, God can use us best. We are not meant to be morally weak, but we are to acknowledge that any good in us is the work of God. Before He can really show His power in and through us we must acknowledge our utter reliance on Him.

In His wisdom, God has deliberately chosen the weak and lowly to shame the strong and wise (1 Corinthians 1:26-39). We have our limitations as earthen vessels, but that which we contain as the gift of God is immeasurable. We are treasure receptacles, filled to overflowing. God has not chosen containers made of durable metal, but jars of clay. Jesus lives and works through weak, afflicted, persecuted, and wearing-out vessels. Those who know they must depend on Him for strength find it while those who think they are strong miss it. We are full of the spirit of faith and the hope of the resurrection and these bear us up in all present tribulation experienced for Jesus' name. What Paul has written is true of all believers who have plunged with abandonment into the true living of the Christian life—the lifestyle of the cross.

Jesus has chosen a very human people. We are not self-sufficient. We have very deep needs. He has chosen ordinary people into which to put the treasure of the gospel. In this way, everyone can see that the change we have undergone, the victory we have, and the life we live are not by our power. God gets the glory.

The treasure we have been filled with is not ours to horde; it is to be shared with everyone. The gospel message is given to us as a trust (see 1 Timothy 6:20 and 2 Timothy 1:14). It is a power-filled message to share and makes possible a power-filled life. That sharing often requires taking risks. In 2 Corinthians 4 Paul gave examples of how suffering was often worked out in the lives of Christians of his day. They were "hard pressed on every side, but not crushed." Paul and his fellow workers experienced the pressure of circumstances and antagonism—pressure from without. The word "crushed" carries the idea of being put in a narrow, cramped place where it is difficult to move. Paul is saying that in the course of obedience to Christ he and others were often pressed hard upon, but never to the point of being totally immobilized.

They were "perplexed, but not in despair." The word "perplexed" means to be at a loss to know what to do or which way to turn. The word for "despair" is the intensive form and means to be utterly without recourse or hope. William Barclay interprets this verse to mean that we may be at our wit's end, but not at hope's end. There are times when a Christian does not know what to do, but still knows that something can be done. We still believe that God is in the situation and will see us through it, that even if our wisdom fails us, God's wisdom will not fail. He is never at a loss. We may not be able to see a long way ahead, but we will emerge from the fog bank into the clear light again. We can never be at hope's end in the presence of Christ, though we may sometimes feel that we have exhausted our own ideas and resources.

Paul mentions being "persecuted, but not abandoned." The word "persecuted" here means to be pursued, harassed, or molested. "Abandoned" means to be left helpless and deserted. The persecuted Christians and martyrs of the early church appeared to have their sweetest times with Christ in the midst of their most troubled circumstances. When they shared in Christ's sufferings they shared in His very presence. So it has been down through the ages. Jesus does not forsake those willing to endure hardship and pain for Him. If we are willing to be unreservedly devoted to Him, we never stand alone. Nothing can alter the loyalty of God. Psalm 27:10 says, "Though my father and mother forsake me, the LORD will receive me." In Matthew 28 Jesus commanded His disciples to take His message to all nations, an endeavor that He had already warned them would result in much opposition (see John 13). But when He gave them this great commission, He added, "And surely I am with you always, to the very end of the age" (Matthew 28:20). We often quote Hebrews 13:5: "God has said, 'Never will I leave you; never will I forsake you.'" But the next verse says, "So we say with confidence, 'The Lord is my helper; I will not be afraid. What can mere mortals do to me?'"

Finally, Paul declares that they were "struck down, but not destroyed." They were cast down, but not ruined or rendered useless (the Greek word for "destroyed" means "to render of no effect"). It is not that Christians never fall under blows, but with the help of God they rise up again. We may take a beating, but we cannot be ultimately defeated as long as we trust in Christ, who won the decisive battle on the cross. After all, did He not appear defeated at His death? But He rose again!

Part of Paul's point in 2 Corinthians 4 is that 1) serving Christ involves running the risk of suffering, and 2) it is worth it. In terms of the lifestyle of the cross, we can put it like this: every committed Christian must constantly live in the spirit of sacrifice. We put our trust in Christ to preserve us if He will. We follow in His footsteps by being willing to go all the way and pay any price to be God's instruments and servants in this kind of world. Though we do not deliberately seek out suffering for ourselves, neither will we run from it if to do so means compromising our relationship with Christ. Our Christian walk and witness must be consistent even in the face of great obstacles. We may not go through persecution and martyrdom of the kind believers in other places experience. We may only meet with mocking, jesting, insults, prejudices, bad jokes, irreverence, labeling, and ostracism. But do not be afraid of these things for nothing can separate us from the love of God. We must be more concerned with pleasing God than pleasing men.

The church must be willing to suffer for Jesus' sake before His life will be made manifest in and through us. Let me emphasize here that Christ's life is not only evident in our suffering, but also when we are not suffering. His life is manifest in our joy and victory and our everyday, ordinary living. However, the presence of that life is still conditional on the *readiness* to stake our very lives on the truth of God. We must be willing to "lose" our lives in order to keep our lives. We must live in His life, or we are only living in ours. This is one of Jesus' conditions of discipleship and an indispensable element of the lifestyle of the cross.

If Christ met with suffering for the gospel, and if we are indeed following His example, we can expect to meet with some kind of suffering as well. As I have stated before in these pages, the church too often formulates programs and priorities that are relatively risk free and that miss or ignore what Jesus wants to do through us in the world. If we become too preoccupied with the opinions of people in the world we find ourselves caving to the world's insistence that we not "push our beliefs down their throat." When they use this phrase they are not commenting on the style of delivery, but insisting on no delivery of the message at all.

(Let me note something parenthetically at this point. The early Christian witnesses argued, pled, and reasoned with others to accept the gospel. There are many examples of this in The book of Acts. The primary Christian mode of witness is to attempt to convince others through a process of discussion and reasoning that the gospel message is true and will meet the needs of people. Other groups, religious and non-religious, attempt to force their opinions on others through military power, economic threats, or by legislation. I believe that the church in America is being persecuted through the latter method in particular. The enemies of the gospel focus much on getting laws passed that will force Christians to accept their way of life and cease from declaring their faith and living according to their conscience. They want to make other opinions illegal. While Christians have advocated for moral laws, they have not tried to do evangelism by legislation. The greater part of the church sees the power of reasonable argument and personal testimony to be the modes of choice in winning others to their way of thinking and living. When a group has to resort to passing laws to force others to accept them, or laws that will silence opposing voices, it indicates that their case is weak and not promotable by reasonable argument. Let the church resist the temptation to return in kind. Stick to declaring the gospel, and if necessary, suffering for the message of the cross. Winning people is one thing; forcing them is another. As Paul declared, the gospel is the power of God to save some.)

For the church, what is at stake is not our convenience, personal preferences, comfort, or even our safety. What is at stake is the winning of souls. We have the message of eternal life. The church must be engaged in no lesser cause than the salvation and discipleship of people.

How often do we as churches make our plans and then ask God's blessing on those plans? The work of the church must be led by *God*. The fellowship of the saints should be characterized by fun, by social events, and by doing proper business. But the overarching purpose must always be the Great Commission. That is the end for every method. The methods (meetings, programs, buildings, and budgets) cannot become the ends. Our reason for being goes far beyond maintaining an organization. It is not primarily about meeting society's expectations of what a church should be. Our mission is life-saving. A spirit of sacrifice is required for ministering to people with a view to both time and eternity. Christian discipleship is about orienting all of life around loving and serving God.

Christian discipleship will expose us to much emotional pressure, perhaps of the kind described by Paul in 2 Corinthians 4. But shall we enjoy salvation and not share that promise with others? Paul's writing reminds us that we must die to self and surrender ourselves over to God's purposes after the manner of Jesus if we want the life of Jesus to be revealed in us. Death and life come in that order in our spiritual lives—death to self brings life in Christ. Death to sin brings abundant life now and forever. Sharing in Christ's suffering leads to sharing in Christ's glory.

Is the authentic life of Christ seen in us? In the church? When the world looks at the church does it see just another religious group carrying out its business of being an organization? Do they see us blandly going about our tasks in an attitude of self-preservation? Or do they see us really living out the message we claim to believe? Is the "business" of the church always God's business (as He sees it) or our business (as we see it)?

I am not suggesting we are doing everything wrong. But we constantly need to check our focus. Perhaps much of what we spend our time on in the church and as individual believers comes short of the lifestyle of the cross.

Someone may say we cannot save souls unless we have a good reputation in society. There is an element of truth to that. The New Testament admonishes us to keep our integrity before the world in order to win the world. We must be loving and caring. But we should also be straightforward about right and wrong, good and evil, heaven and hell. Our frame of reference is not created by society.

Let me suggest that in our attempt to be pleasing to the world we can actually damage our reputation and our message. If there is a disparity between what we say we believe and what we do, the world will see it. We say we believe in heaven and hell and that Christ is the Savior. If we really believe that, the world would expect us to be persuasive. As offensive as the gospel can be to the conscience of sinful men and women, and as much as the world says they do not want religion "forced upon them," there are many people who are hungry for something genuine. Many want something real and perhaps their frustration with us is that we declare great things but don't always live them. Perhaps they want what we believe to be real, but we are not always good examples. Jesus said that all men will know we are His disciples if we love one another. What are they to reasonably believe if they see a church full of internal strife? Perhaps the world doesn't see the church putting souls first, so why should they believe what we do about eternity?

In 2 Corinthians 4:14-18 Paul shared the principles by which he lived the lifestyle of the cross. He knew that the one who shares life with Christ must also share His mission. Christ walked in hostile territory to do God's will. As do we.

Paul was motivated by his hope in the resurrection. He was not interested in saving his life at the risk of finally losing it, for he knew that if death took him God could and would raise him up again. This allowed him to courageously endure any risk. Personal safety and prosperity were not his primary goals. His goal was nothing but obedience to the message of the cross that he declared.

Whatever Paul had to go through, he was more concerned that others be led into God's love and light than with anything else. This concern took priority over his personal comfort. He was not preoccupied with himself, but with Christ's love for him and others. So the church of Jesus' disciples today must be preoccupied with caring about what God really cares about.

Paul knew that his trials were not in vain. He knew that others would benefit now and eternally. Paul's goal was God's goal—the salvation of souls. Nothing else mattered more than this. *This was his great perspective on suffering for Christ's name.*

What is the goal of the church where you worship and serve? Are lesser things getting in the way of God's purpose in and through you? What perspective prevails in your church? Do you help focus your church on God's will or are you a distraction by insisting on your will in your church?

The believer who sets God's concerns above her own interests discovers some exciting things about living. Though her outward body may be worn by afflictions, her inward nature is revived daily by receiving life from God. Her spiritual life testifies about the life of Jesus. She is fed continually. If we focus on the things of God through prayer, Scripture study, and service, our lives will be supernaturally energized beyond anything mere religious activity can accomplish.

In 2 Corinthians 4:17, the word "momentary" does not refer merely to something of short duration, but rather to something that is present now but will pass at some time. It is temporary. The word for "troubles" is the idea of a pressing burden. But the burden that seems to weigh heavy on us now will be exchanged for another weight, the weight of incomparable glory. We can enjoy life now. But there is that glory beyond anything now can offer. Do not let your attention be transfixed by the visible, temporal, sensory things that will pass away. They are very real and not to be ignored, but must be kept in perspective. Temporary problems will give way to eternal peace.

Let me be clear on something. *Affliction is not a way to gain salvation and eternal life.* It is not meant to be a kind of works to earn God's favor. But by a wholehearted love of God we can endure. Afflictions can cause the unregenerate heart to grow bitter, but the regenerated heart is not surprised at what one meets in this world when trying to live for God. Affliction is never a reason to hold back our commitment to serve God.

Jesus told His followers to consider themselves blessed if they undergo rejection for His name, for in this way the prophets and righteous men and women before us suffered. It is nothing new. But we can rejoice and be glad, for our reward is great in heaven.

There is a secret to the endurance of the righteous. Our sufferings are seen as opportunities for inward strengthening. Paul knew that anything he had to suffer in this world could not hold a candle to the glory of heaven if he remained obedient. As Jesus said, "What good is it for someone to gain the whole world, and yet lose or forfeit their very self?" (Luke 9:25).

The promise is this: he who suffers for Christ's cause will share His glory. We don't seek ill-will or suffering. We want to have friends. We would rather those who disagree with our faith always be reasonable and humane in that disagreement. And sometimes that is so, but not always. There is great enmity in the world against the gospel, and we will experience it if we live by the gospel. The only way to avoid the rejection is to live as secret Christians, and Scripture does not allow us that option.

The glory of the church is not in its sufferings, but in the suffering of Christ for it. Only Christ's suffering has redemptive power. But the redeemed will be willing to so identify with the suffering of the Lord for the world that they will be willing to suffer out of love for their Lord. The life the world holds out is valueless compared to the life Jesus offers. Identifying with Jesus' suffering for us means also identifying with His suffering for everyone; and so we know our purpose, our mission.

In glorifying God we de-glorify sin. Jesus said that the things the world esteems God does not esteem. The world might view Christian witnesses as meddlers, interfering with what they want to do. But how will any believe and be saved if those who claim to have the truth do not risk open and persuasive sharing of that truth with those who might spurn them? The life of discipleship is a daring life that speaks the truth in love.

The church is the body of Christ. We are His feet, going where He wants to go. We are His hands held out to a lost world. Jesus risked the displeasure of people every day. As His earthly ambassadors we will run the same daily risk. But the life of Christ will be evidenced in us. Much is at stake and we must fully live the lifestyle of the cross.

Chapter Thirteen

Whatever It Takes

The lifestyle of the cross is the life of total obedience to the person and purpose of Jesus Christ. The prerequisite to living it is the acceptance of Christ as Savior and Lord. Jesus came not to be served, but to serve and to give His life as a ransom for many. The cross means service, and service requires obedience. Since the lifestyle of the cross embodies all the meanings of the life, death, and resurrection of Jesus, the lifestyle of the cross required by Jesus of His disciples is a life of obedience.

Philippians 2:5-11 says, "Have the same mindset as Christ Jesus: Who, being in very nature God, did not consider equality with God something to be used to his own advantage; rather, he made himself nothing by taking the very nature of a servant, being made in human likeness. And being found in appearance as a man, he humbled himself by becoming obedient to death—even death on a cross! Therefore God exalted him to the highest place and gave him the name that is above every name, that at the name of Jesus every knee should bow, in heaven and on earth and under the earth, and every tongue acknowledge that Jesus Christ is Lord, to the glory of God the Father."

In verse five, Jesus is set forth as our supreme pattern. We have looked at other passages that teach us to consider Jesus to be our example in word, action, motivation, purpose, faith, love, and suffering. Here Jesus is put forth as our example in mindset and uncompromising obedience to God.

Jesus declared that He did not come to be served, but to serve and give His life for the ransom of many. His life was one of service—ultimate service. The Son of God deserves our greatest adoration. He did not come to sit comfortably on a throne or to be waited upon. He came to call sinners to repentance and to a salvation He bought with His own blood. He came to associate with outcasts, heal sick bodies, and forgive sins. He taught His followers that the greatest in His kingdom was that one who would be the servant of all. In His last hours He wrapped a towel around His waist and performed the work of a slave—He washed His disciples' feet. And He told them that they should do the same for each other.

Jesus was living the lifestyle of the cross even before He went to the cross. His whole incarnation was for this purpose. He showed us how to live, and He lived as a servant. He was not a doormat by any means, but His motive was to seek the greatest good for people. Peter tried to deny Jesus the chance to wash his feet, but Jesus warned Peter that in saying this He was excluding himself from doing the ministry of the Lord, for in Jesus' act of service Peter was to learn the essence of doing His work. It was equally hard for Peter to comprehend that part of Jesus' service was to be accomplished by dying on a cross. The time was yet to come when Peter would understand the example of His mighty Savior, and that the life of the follower of Christ must also be of the same kind of service. We are not called to die for the sins of others, but in the spirit of Christ's sacrifice we are to serve and conduct our lives in this world.

The world encourages people to seek fame and admiration, power and status. The world values the glory obtained in the doing of a good deed in order to be lauded by others. The world esteems being served above doing the serving and recognition more than compassionate ministry.

Not so the disciples of Jesus. Our aims are not for personal exaltation. Our Master taught us to do our good deeds even when no one sees. Recognition is not the goal of what we do. It feels good when someone notices, but we want to please God above all. While our righteousness should be obvious to the world, it is not because we promote ourselves, but because our lives shine with an unforced light, the light of Jesus Christ living in and through us.

If the Master washed the feet of His followers, what should our attitude be? First of all, our concern is to serve God, and a great part of this is accomplished by serving one another. Jesus exemplified service done in love. His ultimate service of love to us was His death on the cross for our sins.

Paul wrote, "Have the same mindset as Christ Jesus." Jesus' obedience was to His Father. And the love of the Father for us was extended to us and demonstrated to us through His Son. Jesus' obedience was a willing obedience because its motive was love.

Following Jesus' example, our service for one another and for the lost world must never be carried out begrudgingly. We live and act in Christ's name and in His Spirit. Even though He was the eternal Son of God, He did not think Himself above washing His disciples' feet or going to the cross. He did not turn away the crowds saying, "I don't have time right now." Instead, His promise was that He would in no way cast out anyone who came to Him. In fact, with very little time left in His earthly ministry, He spent some of it washing His disciples' feet.

We should be thankful that Jesus did not have the attitude toward God's work and toward us that we sometimes have. He had time and love enough for us. Have this mind in you that is in Christ Jesus. This lifestyle of the cross means service. It is the way Jesus lived on earth. His Spirit lives in us. It is the lifestyle of His disciples who take up their cross and follow Jesus.

The lifestyle of the cross means obedience to God (verse 8).

Think of it! Jesus, the Word of God, through whom the universe was created, came down from the glory of heaven to mingle with those He had made, even taking upon Himself our humanity. Jesus, the Author of life, was obedient to death! He who was not responsible for our sin took our sin and its penalty upon Himself!

Any one of us can refuse to do God's will. Jesus was tempted to be disobedient to His true purpose. To say that Jesus was willingly obedient means that He could have been disobedient if He'd so chosen. He had freedom of choice. A puppet neither obeys nor disobeys, for it is not the puppet who makes the choices about what it is going to do or not do, but rather it is the puppeteer. To say Jesus was obedient even to death means that He willingly chose to obey the Father no matter the cost to Himself. And Paul admonishes us to have the same mind—willingness and purpose—as Jesus Christ. When Jesus said that His followers must take up their cross and follow Him, He made this wholehearted obedience, even in the face of suffering, the condition for being His disciples. The lifestyle of the cross is complete obedience to God no matter what. Is there rejection and persecution? Is their inconvenience? Might we be called upon by God to abandon something that gives us pleasure and doesn't seem bad to us? If so, might we be tempted to swerve from God's purpose for us and design a form of discipleship that makes us happy? Obedience means God commands or asks, and we say yes. And we do so trusting that He has the best plan for our lives, and wants to use us to bring others to Him.

How obedient are you? "Mostly obedient" is not the lifestyle of the cross. Jesus was completely obedient. We need to be constantly growing in our knowledge of God so that our obedience might increase. That implies it might be imperfect right now. But the main thing is that complete obedience is our intention and what we seek. Have we in some ways placed limits on what we will allow God to call upon us to be and do?

What is required, when we are having trouble with obedience, is repentance and a straightforward decision to obey. Any hesitation to give up our preferences will sabotage our decision. With regard to some things, you may already have made up your mind not to obey. You may think God's expectation is unreasonable, and somehow He'll come around. Or you may think, "This isn't so bad. God will understand." Or, "God loves me too much to punish me just for this." This is dangerous, for it is a hardening of the heart. Dear reader, is it possible that in commanding you to abandon something you cannot see as bad God is testing your commitment to obedience? Also, remember that God might call upon you to give up something "good" because while you have it, He cannot give you what is "better" according to His will. A lack of trust in God's love and wisdom will lead us away, even ever so slightly, from the doing of His will. Remember, Jesus our pattern was not mostly obedient, He was completely obedient.

This definite quality in your obedience will be reflected in all things—your prayer life, your commitment to read and study the Bible, your worship, your giving, your witness, your relationships, your job, and your walk in the world. What a difference wholehearted decisions would make in our churches!

"Taking up your cross" translates into wholehearted obedience. There is no option to be a half-hearted disciple of Jesus. He constantly calls us by His authority and example to be completely God's. There is a battle to be waged against evil, and you must take a side. You cannot be on both sides at once. There is a kingdom to be declared and victories to be won in this world. There are souls dependent on our witness. There is no half-hearted soldiering allowed in the army of God. Jesus gave it all on the cross for us. Following Him requires our like commitment to Him and His purposes through us.

Jesus was committed to doing His Father's will, whatever that meant, or cost. The Gospels show us that in those last days before His arrest and crucifixion, Jesus' face was more and more determinedly set toward Jerusalem. The disciples tried to dissuade Him. Peter zealously hindered Him. His family coaxed Him. The Pharisees threatened Him. But Jesus fixed His steps toward the agony of Gethsemane and Golgotha.

The key to Jesus' complete obedience is His love for God and for us. In John 14:28-31, on the evening before He was arrested, Jesus said to His disciples, "You heard me say, 'I am going away and I am coming back to you.' If you loved me, you would be glad that I am going to the Father, for the Father is greater than I. I have told you now before it happens, so that when it does happen you will believe. I will not say much more to you, for the prince of this world is coming. He has no hold over me, but he comes so that *the world may learn that I love the Father and do exactly what my Father has commanded me*." Jesus was motivated and compelled by this love.

Since Jesus is our pattern, the only way we can be as obedient as He was is to have the same motive—our love for God and others. Nothing less will do. This is what defines true, wholehearted, effective, and valuable obedience.

How deeply rooted is your commitment? Would you die for your faith in Christ? Would you die in His service? That consideration may seem far from those of us who live in a free country, so we may take the improbability of facing that for granted. But it is still a valid question. Do we flinch when asked to be involved in some way in God's work that would be hard or risky, or that might bring upon us someone's displeasure? Do we fear to fully love and obey? Do our first thoughts go to ourselves and personal consequences when faced with the opportunity to witness?

Have this attitude among yourselves, which is in Christ Jesus. Christ has shown us loving obedience. He has shown us how. He has told us it involves a cross. This is not necessarily a literal cross we go to. But whatever form our cross takes, it means full obedience to God out of love for Him and others. It will show itself in service to one another and concern for souls. This lifestyle of the cross defines true Christianity. It defines those Jesus recognizes as His disciples.

The lifestyle of the cross sounds hard. But let us not forget its joys—the approval of God, the certainty of heaven, the wonderful fellowship of the saints, the wonder of seeing other lives changed, the experience of pure love and hope. The lifestyle of the cross is lived in everyday ways as well as in exciting adventures. It is the love of God for us, in us, reaching out through us, that makes it thrilling. This is missing from Christian professions that are not lived in wholehearted, "whatever it takes" obedience.

The lifestyle of the cross is a God-directed life. We are in direct contact with God and His love energizes and drives us. We are invulnerable to the enemies of the gospel, for Jesus said those who can kill the body cannot kill the soul. The cross carries the dual meaning of suffering and victory—there is no life more exciting.

Think of the love of Jesus poured out on the cross. He was serving you and me on that cross. What kind of commitment on our part does He deserve? Remember, He did that to save us and make us free, but also to use us to lead others to freedom. Jesus did not die to create another world religion, but to bring His kingdom activity to earth.

Taking Jesus as our example, let us purpose to serve and obey God with all our hearts, which involves serving others wholeheartedly. There will be difficulties doing this in a sinful world, but it is that sinful world we are deliberately engaging in the lifestyle of the cross.

Chapter Fourteen

Enduring the Burden

The Christian life is not static. It must always be going somewhere. We can never stand still in one place. There must be movement, dynamism. And it is not enough that we are merely going "some place." There must be a definite direction, a verifiable course, and a describable goal. The goal of the Christian life is the likeness of Christ. He is ever the pattern to which we are called to attain.

Hebrews 12:1-3 says, "Therefore, since we are surrounded by such a great cloud of witnesses, let us throw off everything that hinders and the sin that so easily entangles. And let us run with perseverance the race marked out for us, fixing our eyes on Jesus, the pioneer and perfecter of faith. For the joy set before him he *endured the cross*, scorning its shame, and sat down at the right hand of the throne of God. Consider him who endured such opposition from sinners, so that you will not grow weary and lose heart."

The Christian life is likened in the Bible to a walk, a stand, a battle, and a race. The basic idea throughout is that Christians are on a definite path to some place. We don't stroll casually through life like tourists, randomly travelling about. We press on toward a specific goal.

In Hebrews 12 the Christian life is compared to a race. To win a race requires determination and consistency. It also requires *endurance*. At times the runner feels weary. Sometimes he may be tempted to give up. But if he is to make it to the finish line and win the prize, he must keep going and not stop. Perhaps the runner will even stumble occasionally, but still must not quit. He must remain in the race or winning is impossible. The racecourse might be full of obstacles and pitfalls, sources of suffering and opposition. There will be those who don't want the runner to win the race and will try to impede him or discourage him. But he must keep running the race or the goal will not be reached.

The words "grow weary" and "lose heart" were used by Aristotle to refer to an athlete who throws himself down on the ground in exhaustion after a grueling race. If he does this before crossing the finish line he loses. The writer of Hebrews is telling his readers not to give up too soon. Jesus spoke of the seed that fell on rocky ground and sprouted quickly, but withered and died when things got too hot. We must finish the race, even when things get hot.

Thank God Jesus didn't give up when things got extremely hard. He endured the suffering. He embraced the cross. Study carefully the race Jesus ran, for He was showing us how to run ours. We might feel too weak to finish, but we need to know that there is a source of strength beyond our own that makes finishing possible. Christ, who endured, lives in us. For Him, the key to that strength was the joy set before Him (our salvation) that enabled Him to endure the burden.

Jesus is described as the "pioneer and perfecter" of our faith, and then His own endurance is described. These two ideas are connected. People of faith are people who pick up their cross and endure its burden, who deny themselves daily, who follow Jesus in the sacrificial and obedient lifestyle of the cross, and who carry the message of the cross to the world near and far.

Jesus is the One who took the lead and showed us the life that pleases God. He showed us the way. He set the example of the life of purpose that is in accord with God's will. Jesus has gone before, and His going before in faith has made faith possible for us who follow. If He is the One we are following, we cannot go wrong. He is the pioneer, the source, the developer, and the perfecter (finisher) of our faith.

It is Jesus we are called on to "consider," that is, to observe as our model and pattern of faith and cross-bearing. We are called upon to examine His motives and purpose, and to act according to the same. We are promised the Spirit of Christ and supported by His strength in living. Let us observe Him who is our example.

Jesus endured much for our salvation. He was continually opposed by sinful people (even religious sinful people). There were the hypocritical Pharisees, the unfaithful Judas, the fickle crowds, the competitive disciples, the pride of Rome. He bore much with sinful men and women. He bore with us until we accepted Him as our Savior. Paul declared that while we were still enemies, Christ loved us and died for us. Jesus still bears patiently with us as we grow in the faith. Taking Him as our example, we also bear with each other, and we endure the antagonism of the world. The necessity of endurance is stated well in Jesus' command that we pick up our cross and follow Him.

Jesus' strong virtues were gentle authority, patience, endurance, persistence, and love that had a mission. This is the example we must live by to be His followers. Our strength lies in our trust in the Lord, and so in the face of any opposition we can continue and not grow too weary and faint. We will not drop out of the race. Even as we work fervently, He gives us rest for our souls. As a racer fixes his eyes on the finish line, we must fix our eyes on Jesus, who is our goal, that we might be like Him and accomplish His will.

We must always keep our eyes fixed on the goal. We must always be looking in the right direction. There are many distractions. Jesus said that the one who begins to plow and looks back is not fit for the kingdom of God. The plowman who looks back and not straight ahead can never make a straight row. The likeness of Jesus is the goal, and so on Jesus we must fix our vision.

Jesus is our Pioneer. He is our Leader in the contest. He has already received the prize and wants us to be co-recipients. He is now seated at the right hand of the Father and wants us to reign with Him. The race is begun with Jesus and must be finished with Him or not at all. And He is there at the finish to award the prize.

Jesus endured every kind of shame that could be inflicted on Him. He was mislabeled, accused, and betrayed. He was yelled at, mocked, spit upon, and beaten. He was tried and falsely found guilty. He was nailed to a cross. He endured all this for the joy set before Him. The joy of obeying the Father. The joy of bringing us into fellowship with Himself. And the joy of the resurrection.

Jesus bore the burden of the cross, a burden greater than most realize, certainly greater than most of us have been willing to bear. Many gospels preached today focus on self-fulfillment, self-improvement, joy, peace, and prosperity. While all of these good things are available in the Christian life, they were made possible through the suffering of Jesus. The gospel message is not complete without urging us to the obedience, sacrifice, and endurance involved in taking up our cross. This was the condition of discipleship Jesus declared. We cannot present a one-sided picture of the Christian life. There are the promises of victory and joy, and also the promises of persecution and endurance.

In John 19:16-18 we read, "Finally Pilate handed him over to them to be crucified.

"So the soldiers took charge of Jesus. Carrying his own cross, he went out to the place of the Skull (which in Aramaic is called Golgotha). There they crucified him."

Close your eyes and envision Jesus carrying the crossbeam of that cross up that hill of Golgotha. Look at Him. Try to see Him. Jesus is bearing His cross, our cross, our sins, our punishment. Look. You can see that rough wooden cross, but can you see your sins and the sins of the world being borne upon His shoulders? He bore our problems, our heartache, our sickness, our greatest trials, our pain, our persecution from the world. He *has* borne it. Do you see it crushing down on Him? We can hardly bear our own, let alone someone else's. He knows and understands it. He has borne the sin that you might be entangled in now. He has already carried it and died so that you can be free from it. The physical cross was not nearly as heavy as the burden of our sins He bore. It was not His sin. It was yours and mine. See how He walks along under your burden all alone. You are not alone. He has borne it and wants you to be free from it, free to walk with Him in victory. Even now He wants to take away your sin and guilt that you might not feel its weight any longer.

Jesus staggered under the load of the cross. He has been without sleep all night. He has been dragged all around Jerusalem, interrogated, tried, mocked, beaten, and bullied. The flesh has been torn from His back by a Roman scourge. Now He bears the weight of a wooden beam, rough and splintery, against His torn back. But it is all for you. It is all that you might not be lost in your sins. It is for your enrichment that He looks so poor. It is for your peace that He is in anguish. It is for your strength that He is so weak. It is to build you up that He is bent down. It is for your freedom that He labors beneath His load. He dies so that you and I might live. Look at Him. Are you afraid to fully face this vision?

Open your eyes. Not only your physical but also your spiritual eyes. The vision has been tragic, but now it turns to victory. The body laid dead in a grave breathes in air again, the heart beats again, the voice speaks again. He rose from the dead to give us His Spirit; now His life continues through us. His ministry of transforming life into death is wrought through His followers.

Jesus bore a cross no other could bear. He alone could carry our sins on the cross. He alone was sinless. Only God in the flesh could offer a sacrifice for all. Being freed from slavery to sin and its guilt, we are now free to enter into His ministry. We do not suffer for our own sins. But desiring to see souls saved will bring us suffering. Jesus wants us to bear with Him His sorrow for every lost soul, and He wants us to bear with Him His great love and desire that all come to believe and have eternal life. In order for others to believe and receive, they must hear the message and see the gospel in real life. That is where we come in.

There is a hymn that asks, "Must Jesus bear His cross alone?" The answer is "Yes." Only He *could* bear that cross. And the answer is "No." The mission started at the cross is not finished until Jesus comes back, and He entrusted that to us with the help of the Holy Spirit. Until He returns, we must carry the message of the cross into the world; not the message of a Christ still on the cross, but of an empty cross and an empty tomb. The cross is not a mystical and magical symbol, but rather the reminder of an historical and present spiritual reality.

Must we bear *our* cross alone? Never! For God has given us each other to bear the burdens of life. He has given us the task of ministry together. (Let us never place divisive burdens on each other, but let us support each other in God's will.) Most of all, He has given us His Holy Spirit, His own living presence to be in us. The living Lord Himself stands beside us and lives within us for the living of the lifestyle of the cross.

The "lifestyle of the cross" is a partnership between us and the living Lord. It is not something we can do alone. It is a "death" and "life" matter for each man and woman in the world. This book has been addressed primarily to disciples. It is an urgent call to give your all to Christ and for a lost world. Only one kind of discipleship will meet Christ's approval and help us be effective Christians in this world. I pray that the chapters of this book will convince each reader of the true definition of discipleship, the joy of total commitment, and the importance of the lifestyle of the cross to the effectiveness of Christian living and the church's mission in the world.

Remember this: your sins are not your cross. Jesus' cross is about taking away your sins and ending sin's domination in your life.

Your human weaknesses are not your cross, though they make necessary your complete reliance on the strength of God.

The cross you are to carry is your complete identification with the death and resurrection of Jesus Christ so that you enter into them by faith. The lifestyle of the cross is the living of a life made possible by Jesus' life and death. And the cross you carry is the message of the cross. It will soften the hearts of some and harden the hearts of others. This lifestyle of identification and obedience and this message constitute the cross you are to carry as you walk in this world. It will seem light at times and heavy at times, but the joy of endurance is never absent. Jesus staggered under your load of sin. We can bear His life into the world through our unencumbered lives. The burden we now need to bear is a purposeful one, a redemptive one. He wants to bear you in His arms along the way.

APPENDIX

Outline and Scriptural Basis for the Lifestyle of the Cross

I. THE CROSS OF CHRIST
   A. Use and symbolism.
      1. A horrible symbol of the worst death.
      2. Not unique. Thousands were crucified by the Romans and others.
      3. Became a beloved symbol even during the time it was still being used. This is one proof of the reality of Christ's resurrection.
      4. Still represents suffering, sacrificial love, and God's redemptive plan.
   B. Scriptures regarding the suffering of the cross.
      1. Matthew 20:19—Jesus unjustly abused.
      2. John 19:17—Jesus bore His own cross.
      3. Hebrews 12:2—Endurance and shame.
      4. Philippians 2:8—Obedience.

II. THE MESSAGE OF THE CROSS
   A. 1 Corinthians 2:2—The cross is central to the Christian message. It is the sole basis for preaching and conduct. See also Galatians 3:1.

- B. 1 Corinthians 1:8—The message of the cross is foolishness to the world.
- C. 1 Corinthians 1:23—The message of the cross is an offense to the world.
- D. Galatians 5:11—The offense of the cross.
- E. 1 Corinthians 1:17—Human wisdom dilutes the message.
- F. 1 Corinthians 1-3—The wisdom of God versus the wisdom of man. Believers are conductors of this divine wisdom.

III. OUR CROSS
- A. Matthew 10:38; 16:24—Christ's definition of and conditions for genuine discipleship.
- B. Romans 6:6—The old self is crucified.
- C. Galatians 2:20—We are crucified with Christ. Christ is living through us.
- D. 2 Corinthians 13:3—Crucified in weakness, living in power.
- E. Romans 6:5-12; 7:4-6; 8:3-6,10,18; 12:1-2; 13:14—Freedom from sin.
- F. 1 Peter 4:1-5,12-19.

IV. CHRISTIAN LIFESTYLE—application and priorities
- A. 2 Corinthians 4:7-18.
- B. Philippians 2:8—Obedience.
- C. Ephesians 2:16—Unity.
- D. Matthew 5 and Hebrews 11—Endurance of persecution.
- E. Romans 8:18; James 1:2-4; 2 Corinthians 4:8; Romans 5:3; Hebrews 10:36; 1 Corinthians 4:12; 9:12; 2 Timothy 2:10; 3:12; James 1:12—Endurance for Christ's sake. The inevitability of suffering for Christ.
- F. Galatians 6:14—The world crucified to me.

www.ingramcontent.com/pod-product-compliance
Lightning Source LLC
Chambersburg PA
CBHW021440080526
44588CB00009B/621